A Sociological Yearbook
of Religion in Britain · 2

Edited by David Martin

SCM PRESS LTD

This book has been produced in co-operation with
Socio-Religious Research Services

334 01554 5

First published 1969
by SCM Press Ltd
56 Bloomsbury Street London WC1

© *SCM Press Ltd 1969*

Printed in Great Britain by
Billing & Sons Limited
Guildford and London

CONTENTS

Contents

THE CONTRIBUTORS

ERIC BUTTERWORTH   Senior Research Fellow in Community Organization, University of York

COLIN CAMPBELL   Lecturer in Sociology, University of York

KENNETH DEMPSEY   Lecturer in Sociology, University of New England, Armidale, New South Wales, Australia

MARTIN GOODRIDGE   Lecturer in Sociology, Bingley College of Education, Bingley, Yorkshire

MICHAEL HILL   Assistant Lecturer, London School of Economics and Political Science

ROBIN JENKINS   Fellow in the Department of Sociology, University of Essex

ALASDAIR MACINTYRE   Professor of Sociology, University of Essex

ROBERT TOWLER   Assistant Lecturer in Sociology, University of Leeds

BRYAN TURNER   Department of Social Studies, University of Leeds

PETER WAKEFORD   Senior Programmer, Computer Services Unit, London School of Economics and Political Science

T. RENNIE WARBURTON   Associate Professor, University of Victoria, British Columbia, Canada

Apologies are offered to Dr W. S. F. Pickering, Senior Lecturer in Sociology at Newcastle University, for an incorrect description of his post in the first issue of the *Yearbook*.

PREFACE

IT WOULD be pleasant to think that the first issue of this yearbook demonstrated the usefulness of regularly collecting material on religion in Britain. There is not much difficulty in finding enough material to make up such collections, although it now appears that there is unlikely to be a sufficient number of articles at any particular time to plan issues thematically. Of course if it were possible to commission research, or direct it oneself for a longish period, then a yearbook could reflect a co-ordination of interest. Unfortunately just as one must take research students as they come and co-operate with their research concerns, so one must take the subjects of articles as they come. It was at least hoped to concentrate this edition on the migrant religious groups in Britain, but for various reasons only the article by Eric Butterworth witnesses to that original intention.

However, that may not really be so much of a loss: a number of reviewers welcomed the eclectic character of the last issue. Two of the articles on Methodism are justified not only intrinsically but because they concentrate on the immediate issue of ecumenicalism. Taken together they are a profitable addition to our understanding and a useful addendum to Robert Currie's work on ecumenical movements within Methodism. The third article on Methodism – that by Kenneth Dempsey – is an example of a genre the editor has previously advocated: a micro-study which does not omit the wider confessional milieu. Robin Jenkins' contribution on Northern Ireland reminds us of the mutual interaction of religion and politics. The sociology of religion is too often practised in isolation, and its most immediate and proper relation is surely to the sociology of politics. A point common to Hill, Turner, Dempsey and Jenkins is the element of conflict between religious professionals (especially over ecumenicalism) and a section of the active laity in the local church. Similar conflict would also arise from a difference between local political opinion and the (often radical) pronouncements of the Church's specialized agencies: one says 'would', because local opinion is normally ignorant of what the specialized agencies are saying.

T. Rennie Warburton provides a contribution in the tradition established by Bryan Wilson of careful institutional analysis focused on the smaller type of sectarian or semi-sectarian community. Robert Towler's work on the ministry complements the articles by Michael Daniel and Eric Carlton[1] in the *Yearbook* for 1968 on this topic of grave concern to the Church and continuing interest to sociologists interested in the professions.

Two articles on humanism and communism respectively are defensible in terms of another editorial predilection: for linking up the sociology of religion to belief systems in general. So far as Colin Campbell's piece is concerned it reminds us that humanism has its specific – and limited – milieu, and it may also be useful to recollect that progressive attitudes amongst humanist leaders are by no means reflected amongst the broader mass of non-religious in Britain.[2] It may seem that Alasdair MacIntyre's approach is essentially philosophical rather than sociological but in fact his essay appears in this volume as illustrating the degree of interpenetration between the two spheres, or at any rate the indefiniteness of the boundary between them. Furthermore, it is concerned with ecumenical feeling at its most catholic. The first Christian-Marxist dialogue in Britain took place some eighteen months ago.

Goodridge's work on Bristol represents an essay in transplanting the French approach to the historical sociology of religion in terms of a careful assessment of local evidence about religious practice area by area. Such a transplantation follows a similar operation performed in the sphere of historical demography – incidentally a type of study which also has its importance for the study of religion in Britain. Goodridge's piece links naturally enough with John Gay's contribution on religious geography in the first issue.

To conclude this preliminary survey it may be worth reminding readers of how the yearbook came into existence. Bryan Wilson's institutional analyses of sects, Anthony Spencer's charting of the Roman Catholic Church, Leslie Paul's proposals for the administrative restructuring of the Church of England together produced a burgeoning of interest amongst two publics: sociologists and informed Christians. One of the most favourably received articles in the first issue, Kenneth Thompson's on Bureaucracy in the Anglican Church, developed themes followed by Wilson and implicit in Leslie Paul's Report – themes which were indeed debated between them in *Theology*.

My own book in turn tried to summarize evidence of varying quality and to suggest future lines of research. I was acutely conscious of the holes in that evidence and of the fact that I had only cut one slanted tunnel into the mysterious Silbury Mound of English religion. The evidence needed filling out, other slants were required: hence the yearbook. And I wanted it to cover the field in the manner already indicated: avoiding the isolation of religion as a separate sociological concern, joining it with studies of politics and ideology, attacking the subject at every level from the intimate interaction of small communities to the political stance of specialized ecclesiastical agencies, and tying religion in with all the kinds of work currently done on modern Britain, whether it be on birth control practices in a journal like *Population Studies* or on religiously coloured youth movements like the Boy Scouts.[3]

NOTES

1. Michael Daniel, 'Catholic, Evangelical and Liberal in the Anglican Priesthood', *A Sociological Yearbook of Religion in Britain*, 1968, pp. 115–23; Eric Carlton, ' "The Call": the Concept of Vocation in the Free Church Ministry', *ibid.*, pp. 106–14.

2. Bernice Martin, 'Comments on Some Gallup Poll Statistics', *Yearbook*, 1968, p. 148.

3. Cf. J. Sinclair, 'Charisma and the Monolithic Nature of Scouting' (based on an M.A. thesis in social anthropology at Edinburgh), *SAGGA* (Scout and Guide Graduate Association) *Journal* 6, April 1968, pp. 2–21; also V. W. R. Markham, 'Membership of Youth Movements in Great Britain', *ibid.*, 4, October 1967, pp. 2–6.

INTRODUCTORY COMMENT

SOCIOLOGICAL investigation in general proceeds at several levels, empirical, structural and phenomenological. It uses various techniques all the way from statistical correlation to the process of indicating the propriety of a certain constellation of attitudes for a particular social structure. The sociology of religion obviously proceeds at the same levels and employs an equal range of techniques. In this short comment I want to indicate certain problems largely occurring at opposite ends of the scale: from empirical relationships and factual description to certain broad types of enquiry relating to the social context of past and future sensibility. Indeed one might say I wanted to indicate the sense and the sensibility of the sociology of religion.

Quantitative enquiry and factual description are notoriously threadbare and inadequate in themselves, inasmuch as they require a whole apparatus of explanatory models and interpretative 'grips'. (This is, of course, quite separate from the incidental difficulty of the psychological insensitivity and philosophical *naïveté* of some empirically minded investigators – a painful subject, but hardly an inherent methodological problem.) These methods also raise awkward questions of veracity and the relation of mere fact to the 'real situation', as well as creating a gap between themselves and the broader accounts of the ebb and flow of ideas and literary re-creations of particular social atmospheres.

The question of veracity is fairly simple at one level. When, for example, I report poll findings which state that 25% attended church in a month, people are either speaking the truth, misremembering, or lying. (Unfortunately I know of no investigation of lying habits: would such an investigation have to discount the reports of those who said they were heavy liars, or could it give them weight?) The question relates to an objective situation which can be checked provided certain criteria for the activity in question are set up. On the other hand when I report that over four in five 'believe in God' I refer in an over-simple manner to an issue which is complicated by the range of meanings attached to 'belief' and to 'God' and furthermore by the way such a 'belief' is woven into the fabric of people's views, attitudes and actions. Nor can I improve the situation very much by producing more theologically sophisticated but unusable questionnaires: one can only know such things by personal confrontation of individuals and by perambulating around their belief system to see how it works in various contexts.

What I am driving at may be illustrated by a curious incident occurring while a group of students at the London School of Economics conducted an enquiry into superstition and belief in Islington. One student located a man who appeared totally indifferent to religious practice and belief until asked whether he believed in God. He paused, and then said that he had once been on a jury and had taken the oath, hence he must believe in God since if he did not he ought to have admitted it at the time. Presumably he meant that Someone kept a note of such matters and once on the 'books' one could hardly get the entry erased. Identical, but more frequent, difficulties arise when people say, 'Yes, I'm a Christian – I mean I'm not a heathen.' What range of implication is involved in 'not being a heathen'?

The 'range of implication' involved in one apparently simple empirical question relates to the whole issue of a general ethos. It is extraordinarily difficult to bring the two levels into vital and extensive relationship, and even more difficult to relate them both to the category of historical 'event'. For example, an important part of the general psychological history of this country is the watershed created by the event of the First World War.[1] The War set off moods, attitudes, indifferences, commitments of all kinds, dislocations, which must have had an impact on religious practice. But it is almost impossible to locate and verify the broad tendencies set in being by such an 'event' as the War for the institutional practice of the Church, especially its statistical state of health. Indeed, the whole category of historical 'event' can barely be related – in the contemporary sociology of religion – to quantitative evidence. (Perhaps this is peculiarly difficult in Britain. In other countries it may be easier: in Indonesia, for example, the empirically verifiable expansions in Christianity after the 'event' of the Muslim-Communist massacres allows connections to be made, even though the explanations do involve guesses controlled by very loose criteria.) Political sociology is full of events trailing quantitative empirical consequences, but the nearest religious sociology moves to an event is a long-term trend.

Not only is there this gap between trends in (fairly) hard evidence
and modifications in the general ethos but there is also a gap between
such evidence and intellectual history, including the history of theological movements. It is assumed that intellectual history has some
importance outside itself as simply the inside story of the intelli-
gentsia just as theology is more than the cerebrations of different
assortments of clergy: both are believed to be refracted in the social
system at large, including the church. But it is not at all easy to
bring together questions concerned (say) with neo-orthodoxy, the
influence of tractarian ideas, or even the statistically accountable
popularity of the Bishop of Woolwich's *Honest to God* with such an
account of the sociology of English religion as I have attempted to
give myself.[2] Or to take general intellectual history, people write
broadly about religion and the twentieth century and (say) the
impact of the Freudian revolution but it is not at all easy to see
what this impact was, or whether it had any important impact at all.
Those who use such phrases may only be speaking about the experience of their own very limited circle.

Indeed, we know relatively too much about the articulate strata
and what we know is too often in terms of strikingly talented authors
or in terms of new movements which neglect the persistent inertias
and unadvertised majorities. (The Church of England, for example,
has an odd way of surviving, even ignoring, any number of intellectual cross-currents and theological fashions.) What we do *not*
know is the ethos of various religious milieux conceived as styles of
living. While we have portraits of national character and even of its
generalized religious component we have few portraits of what it is
like to be a Congregationalist, or an Irish Catholic member of the
lower middle class.[3] No doubt journalists and novelists might write
about Irish navvies, but the picture would be highly coloured and
probably distorted. Our picture of Puritanism, for example, is
almost entirely a vicious journalistic fiction.

When I use a phrase like 'style of living' I mean such matters as
the wise saws most current, or what is characteristically seen as an
appropriate range of obligation. Another area is that of daily ritual,
when to eat, when to retire at night. Again, what are the degrees of
acceptable cleanliness, and punctuality, what is regarded as an
'occasion', which events are seen as provoking reprisal? For
example, I have the impression that Free Churchmen do not know
quite how *legitimately* to express anger and resentment. All such

items make up a way of life. They call for imagination in connecting them together and also in relating them to the social status structure in which they occur and come to be regarded as 'normal'. Such styles require phenomenological approaches as well as structural analysis.

The question of the employment of a phenomenological method alongside empirical methods and structural analysis allows one to move on and point to a whole range of quite different problems glanced at in the article by Alasdair MacIntyre: they certainly lead to philosophical questions of some magnitude. For example, there is the connection frequently posited between the mundane success of an ideology or religion and its truth. There are plenty of people, including clerics, who feel some relationship must exist between declines in institutional Christianity and its falsity, or at any rate false accretions obscuring its true essence. Sociology on the other hand substitutes the notion of structural propriety to account for success or failure in given milieux: a substitution which runs into serious difficulties with the – admittedly overestimated – spread of science and scientific method and also into some milder difficulties with an ideology like Marxism which itself employs both the notion of 'propriety' to explain its differential social success *and* the notion of truth in so far as a given structure or stratum is differentially open to the truth. (The notion runs parallel to the evangelical dictum: 'the humble poor believe'.)

The overlap between philosophy and sociology also becomes clear when we try and isolate what form of 'system' Christianity is: is it, for example, parallel to Marxism, or in a different category, or only partly different? This is an important issue for Professor MacIntyre's argument. Clearly Christianity has been largely relieved of the incubus of out-of-date science: in that sense demythologization is well advanced. And sociology helps us here by suggesting that the component of out-of-date science was not historically the element of 'appeal', and therefore that the question of the rivalry of religion with science is only marginally related to declines. No doubt certain intellectually sensitized people who live in the 'interim period' between outmoded attempts to produce integrated world-pictures of a religio-scientific kind and the separation out of empirical science on the one part and religion on the other suffer severe distress. But the 'separated out' Christianity relates to questions and to modes of apprehension which are not in principle subject to scientific adjudication any more than are questions of ethics or aesthetics. In other words, we can say: (*a*) the question of 'truth' is not important for sociological understanding or for projections of the historical fortunes of Christianity; and (*b*) Christianity is in any case not basically a set of verifiable or falsifiable assertions. Rather is it a form of 'solid poetry': a style of interpretation, a mode of celebration, a type of responsibility and discipline, a way of focusing certain existential constituents of hope, tragedy and despair, and an integrated symbolism for all these things. (In saying this, I do not mean that Christianity does not embody *assertions*, for example, about the finality of death, but these seem to me the object not of empirical verifications and falsifications but of more or less persuasive and coherent considerations. Biblical historicity is too complex to be entered into here, especially as it is linked to the question of the Resurrection.) The question then becomes: what have been the structural locations of this system and its variants in the past, and what are the structural possibilities – if any – so far as we can see them in the future. What limitations and openings have operated on and for this system and what will operate for generations to come?

One can be clearer and less contentious by giving an example from another culture and another religion. A little while ago I participated in the climax of an act of Muslim worship in Southern Bulgaria: naturally I asked myself whether an attitude of total self-abasement had any future, given what we know about likely configurations in the psycho-historical process; and I was inclined to see it as fatally culture-bound. So now we ask what structural developments in *our* society and their associated psychologies are capable of any fruitful union with the socio-psychology of Christianity given the configuration of emphases and 'faults' bequeathed us by the heaving geological pressures of the past two centuries. And to do this requires the phenomenological imagination as well as structural analysis.[4]

Let us suggest the history of Christianity in this period of upheaval through a simple image: unwanted pregnancy. The Christian religion under the influence of industrialism has been impregnated – not of course for the first time – by foreign bodies which activate what is already latent and yet subject the body of the Church to processes outside its control and tear the maternal fabric. A new social body is freed from the institutional framework of the Church and yet contains elements from the original matrix, some recognizable, others totally fused with the character of the paternal agents. Christianity

is now a house-bound crippled institutional matrix – *corpus Chris-
tianum* – and an inchoate, suffused, semi-identifiable set of elements
in a new form of social organization. Now as sociologists we have to
abandon the simple identification of Christianity with *corpus Chris-
tianum*, and identify as far as we can these elements spilt, inchoate,
formless in modern society. I mean varieties of incipient awareness,
formless mysteries, reverences, unfocused rejoicings, occasions
which seem to point beyond themselves without explicit religious
language or sacramental expression; or alternatively all the dis-
jointed modern analogues of theological categories which carry new
paternal names to disguise their maternal origin.[5]

Two broad queries suggest themselves. First a general one: is the
original integrated matrix of any more use; i.e., what role remains
for Mother Church? Second, what are the structural possibilities
which make such a role viable? The first question is about a re-
integration, in institutions and in sensibility, which can at least
viably coexist with (and perhaps continue to fructify or affect) the
vagrant sensibilities already referred to. Is it that the moment of
birth irremediably outdated the corporate framework of Mother
Church? Or was it that a break was necessary but not a death? Were
we separated from a *particular* class culture at a moment of exacer-
bated class relations and divisive cultural differentiation or are we
separated from the very notion of integrated cultures of a religious
type (or at any rate cultures informed in some way by major religious
institutions)? Can the formless be given a form, the uncalled-for
'moments' an hour and a time, the intimation a discipline, the categories an explicit and overall relation, the symbols a universal
relevance?

I can only hint at the structural analysis necessary to begin the
second question. The development of dependence and independence
needs analysing, to see what place 'dependencies' can have and
should have in the psychology of the future. How do these dependencies relate to those encapsulated in the Christian religion? Or
again, does the erosion of the congealed, constipated male psychology which was embarrassed by religious awareness and concomi-
tantly the erosion of the domesticated enclosed femininity which
deformed religion in its own image, allow a healing of the split which
has occurred along sexual lines over institutional practice and
sensibility? A further example can be found in Alasdair MacIntyre's
own remark about the confusion over what constitutes a good life

and a good death. Since presumably Christianity would require some definition of these things, can we imagine how means of communication, with their dominant archetypes, how the models offered by educational agencies, and the diversifying effects of widely different roles, the consequences of considerable leisure, plenty and so on might allow or disallow the establishment of such a definition? This is the question hinted at in the phrase current at the Uppsala Conference 'Towards a new style of living'. Finally, given such likely patterns of work and leisure, what ought logically to be the dominant problematics to which they give rise, and would these operate so as to exclude or facilitate the problematics of religion?

It is questions such as these which ought legitimately to be included in the work of the sociological imagination.

NOTES

1. For some of the linking evidence which might be cited, see S. Mews, *The Effects of the First World War on English Religion and Life*, M.A. thesis, Leeds, 1967.

2. J. A. T. Robinson, *Honest to God*, London: SCM Press, 1963; D. A. Martin, *A Sociology of English Religion*, London: SCM Press and Heinemann, 1967.

3. John Vincent in *The Formation of the Liberal Party* (London: Constable, 1966) makes precisely this point in relation to religion in the nineteenth century.

4. It requires the sort of imagination found, for example, in Philip Rieff's book *The Triumph of the Therapeutic* (New York: Harper, and London: Chatto and Windus, 1964)—though not his sort of conclusions.

5. See my editorial contribution, 'The Dissolution of the Monasteries', to *Anarchy and Culture: the Problem of the Contemporary University*, London: Routledge and Kegan Paul, 1969.

1 Disembodied Ecumenicalism: A Survey of the members of Four Methodist Churches in or near London[1]

Michael Hill and Peter Wakeford

THE FOLLOWING article is the preliminary report on a survey of Methodists in an area south of London. We have concentrated in the initial stage of analysis on an investigation of attitudes towards ecumenicalism in general and towards the Church of England in particular.

Survey and questionnaire design

With the support of the Connexional Church Membership Committee and the Home Mission Department of the Methodist Church, and with the co-operation of ministers in the churches involved, a mailed questionnaire was sent to members[2] of four churches in or near London in September, 1967. The churches chosen were Byfleet, Crawley, Forest Hill and Upper Norwood. These were selected because they represented different areas in and around London: two adjacent suburbs, the commuter belt and a New Town. Three of them had a total membership figure of between 200 and 280 and the fourth had just under 200 members; in this way we hoped to control one of the variables influencing 'effectiveness'.[3] Since the questionnaire contained items on the spouse and children of the respondent it was sent to one member of a family. Where only one individual in a household was a Methodist member it was sent to that person, and where husband and wife were both members the questionnaire was sent to the husband. Distribution was through the churches and arrangements were made for completed questionnaires to be returned through the churches or sent direct to the research team in an addressed envelope. Every household in which there was a member belonging to one of the four churches received a questionnaire. The total number of questionnaires sent out was 557, of which 328 were returned, giving a response rate of 59%. The separate response rates for the four churches varied between 55% and 65%. There was no follow-up of non-respondents.

The questionnaire included items on the demographic characteristics of the respondent and the respondent's spouse, children, father and spouse's father. Sex, age, education, further education and occupation were asked for, and as far as occupation was concerned it seems from a preliminary glance at the data that we can confirm the pattern of upward social mobility among Methodists.[4] There were sections on religious practice – average attendance and membership of various organizations – and on respondents' attitudes to other churches. In the section dealing with ecumenicalism we also asked respondents what they thought were important aspects of worship and belief. Since there had already been an enquiry into the attitudes of Methodist *leaders* to this question[5] we thought that by using a similar wording we might obtain useful comparative data.

There are two questions which provide the basis for most of the tabulations in this article. The first asked: 'Do you think that Christians of different denominations should aim for unity or do you think there is some value in having different Christian churches?' There was a choice of three responses: 'Should aim for unity', 'Differences valuable' and 'Difficult to say'. The question which followed asked, 'What would be your opinion on the Methodist Church uniting with the following Christian groups? Do you think it would be a good thing or a bad thing?' Five responses were possible (very good, good, undecided, bad, very bad) for each denomination in a list of nine – the Church of England, Baptists, Roman Catholic Church, Congregationalists, Presbyterians, Salvation Army, Quakers, Unitarians and Elim Pentecostal. Clearly, the answers we got must be interpreted in the light of differential information about these groups and the extent to which unity with a particular group was immediately likely or purely hypothetical. This emerged in the non-response against each denomination, with the Church of England having the highest number of responses given. Perhaps our categories were too restricted: on one memorable questionnaire a respondent had added 'impossible' after 'very bad' in order to register his attitude to unity with the Roman Catholic Church.

Social characteristics of the 328 respondents

60% of our respondents were male and 40% female, since husbands always received questionnaires for the whole family when they were members. This means that the proportion of female members is markedly under-represented, though we can offer projections as to how this might affect the overall results. The only church in which there was a noticeable difference in the proportion of male to female respondents was Byfleet, where only 20% of responses were from females. This may partly account for some of the attitudinal differences which we will discuss later. The other churches conformed more closely to the overall distribution, except that there was some tendency for the two inner-London churches to be split more on a 50–50 basis.

24% of the total were single, 63% married, 11% widowed, 1% separated and 1% divorced. As we might expect, the two suburban churches, Forest Hill and Upper Norwood, had a significantly higher proportion of single respondents, and in fact were almost identical in pattern, with around half of the total married, one-third single and one-sixth widowed. Byfleet and Crawley were almost identical too, with just over three-quarters married, one-sixth single and the remainder mainly widowed.

The age structure of the sample is shown in Table 1. (All figures in the tables are percentages unless otherwise stated.)

Table 1 AGE STRUCTURE OF THE FOUR CHURCHES

Age groups	Byfleet	Crawley	Forest Hill	Upper Norwood	Total
15–19	8	3	2	14	7
20–29	6	12	12	11	10
30–39	22	33	13	12	20
40–49	23	28	12	19	20
50–59	19	9	16	11	14
60–69	14	9	25	16	16
70 and over	8	6	20	17	13
Total	100	100	100	100	100
(Total number)	(84)	(78)	(85)	(81)	(328)

Despite the probability that we have underestimated the figures for the 70+ age group (invalids and those who found the questionnaire difficult) there is a clear difference here between the New Town church and the others, with a larger proportion of respondents in the 30–50 age group. The inner-London suburban churches tend to have an older age structure; yet Upper Norwood seems to contain a greater number of young people who were not children of church members and Forest Hill has a somewhat 'older' membership. The fact that we have not shown children of members who were themselves members will, of course, influence these figures, but in fact this involved a similar figure of around 15 in each church so there is a consistent difference for each church.

Only 9% of our respondents had manual jobs. 26% were classified as lower white-collar workers (junior non-manual and personal service workers) and 33% came in the intermediate non-manual group, generally in occupations ancillary to professions. 20% were in employer, managerial and professional occupations. Of the remainder, 6% were housewives and 6% gave no response. We were dealing therefore with an overwhelmingly middle-class group. In none of the separate churches was the percentage of manual workers higher than 13%. Byfleet had slightly more manual workers – being near a large aircraft factory – but the difference was slight. Forest Hill and Upper Norwood contained noticeably higher proportions of junior non-manual workers. Again, the split comes between Byfleet/Crawley and Forest Hill/Upper Norwood: the churches in each pair are remarkably similar. This was somewhat surprising in view of the myths we had heard about Surrey stockbrokers; in fact Upper Norwood had most employers and managers and Byfleet had the highest proportion of professionals.

It seems also that our respondents had experienced a higher level of education than the population at large. 50% said they had attended grammar, independent, comprehensive or pre-war secondary schools, 28% elementary schools, 9% technical or commercial schools; 13% were unclassified or gave no response. The figures for each church are given in Table 2.

The most striking difference in educational experience is between elementary and grammar school attendance. While 17–18% of the Byfleet/Crawley respondents had last attended elementary school, the figure for Forest Hill/Upper Norwood was 28–29%. The corresponding figures for grammar school attendance were 46% as against 34% and 31% for the two suburban churches.

Further education of some sort was quite common. 13% had

attended university, 6% teacher training college, and 27% had had some form of professional or technical training after leaving school. 28% definitely stated they had gone on to further education after school, 15% had taken unclassified courses and 11% gave no response. Table 3 breaks these figures down for separate churches.

Table 2 EDUCATIONAL EXPERIENCE IN THE
FOUR CHURCHES

Last School attended	Byfleet	Crawley	Forest Hill	Upper Norwood
Elementary	17·9	16·7	29·4	28·4
Comprehensive	—	3·8	1·2	7·4
Grammar/pre-war Secondary	46·4	46·2	34·1	30·9
Secondary Modern	8·3	6·4	1·2	3·7
Technical	9·5	14·1	1·2	4·9
Commercial	1·2	1·3	2·4	3·7
Independent (direct grant and public)	8·3	3·8	8·2	8·6
Other and no reply	8·4	7·7	22·4*	12·3

* included several Central Schools

Table 3 FURTHER EDUCATION IN THE
FOUR CHURCHES

Further education	Byfleet	Crawley	Forest Hill	Upper Norwood
None	22·6	25·6	34·1	28·4
Apprenticeship	8·3	7·7	1·2	1·2
Professional	14·3	9·0	9·4	9·9
Technical	15·5	16·7	5·9	8·6
Teacher training	2·4	10·3	8·2	4·9
University	14·3	11·5	12·9	12·3
Other	14·3	11·5	15·3	19·8
No reply	8·3	7·7	12·9	14·8

Perhaps the most important single feature in the four churches was the consistently high proportion of university-educated respondents. In every case between 11 and 14% of respondents said they had attended university. Respondents in the two suburban churches tended to include a greater proportion of people who had gone on to no further education, which may be partly at least a function of the higher proportion of female respondents in these cases. Crawley had the highest proportion of teacher training college graduates – 10% – and Byfleet the lowest – 2%.

The average number of children for each married or once-married respondent was 1·9, which is very near the national average of 2·3: one would certainly expect a figure slightly below 2·3 if we allow for social class and for the fact that among the widows there were almost certainly some with uncompleted families. No respondent had more than 5 children. There was little difference between the four churches. Byfleet had an average of 2·1 children per family, only slightly above the overall average. Together with the data on occupation the figures on family size do suggest that, despite some differences in the areas from which the churches drew their members, we are dealing with a group of individuals who share certain basic characteristics.

A question on political attitudes found that there was a relatively high proportion of Liberals among our respondents. The percentage preferences for each political party were: Conservatives, 32%; Liberals, 31%; Labour, 19%; no preference, 12%; others and no reply, 6%. The highest proportion of Liberals was at Crawley (44%) and the lowest in Upper Norwood (22%), and this was the only noticeable variation between the four churches. The Liberal/Free Church/Friendly Society nexus has, of course, been well-documented by Stacey,[6] but the proportion of Liberals in our sample is surprisingly high. One might perhaps expect a greater number of Liberals in a New Town, where the institutional network is more fluid and less likely to have crystallized on traditional party lines.

Religious background and observance

In the question on parental and baptismal denominations only two churches were significantly represented and these were the Methodist Church and the Church of England. The percentage distribution of these groups is given in Table 4.

Table 4 RELIGIOUS HISTORY OF RESPONDENTS

| | Denomination of respondent's | | |
	father	mother	baptism
Methodist	37	40	38
Church of England	34	37	37

No other denomination had a figure higher than 8% under any heading, though interestingly enough the denomination of next importance was the Baptist Church, and here we are faced with the problem of how our respondents defined baptism. What these figures show, however, is that the Methodist Church and the Church of England between them accounted for some three-quarters of the 'family background' of the Methodist respondents, in almost equal proportions. There was hardly any difference in this pattern in the four separate churches.

23% of our respondents said that almost all of their relatives were Methodist members, 51% said some and 25% said none. In other words, just under a quarter of our respondents came from what might be labelled 'traditional' Methodist families. There was some difference between the individual churches on this point. The percentage of those who said that almost all of their relatives were Methodist members was twice as high in Byfleet as it was in Upper Norwood – 31% as against 16%. But the church with the highest proportion of respondents who had no Methodist relatives was Crawley (33%).

What the above data on parental/baptismal and family denomination suggest is that Methodism recruits only partially through birthright membership. The implications of this for a typology of Christian organizations can only be loosely drawn, but one would expect a church-type organization to recruit fairly extensively through birthright membership and a sect-type organization principally to recruit specifically committed adults. In practice this distinction cannot be made too rigorously[7] but other evidence from this survey supports the belief that the conscious choice of adults to join Methodism is a significant element in recruitment. Several respondents wrote comments on their questionnaires which revealed a specific commitment to Methodism, for example:

> I think that the Methodist services are much more down-to-earth than the Church of England. I feel a real part of it, whereas in the Church of England I felt nothing; in fact I felt that I didn't really belong.

On the other hand, there was little evidence of *exclusive* commitment, and in one (as yet untabulated) question on respondents' religious life-histories there was evidence of considerable 'shopping around', particularly when people moved and found no place of worship belonging to their previously-attended denomination in the area. Thus the group of respondents we are considering do not seem to fit too well into either the church-type or the sectarian pattern, and we cite this as evidence supporting the categorization of Methodism as a denomination.[8]

70% said they attended a place of worship on average once or twice a week – 77% had attended 'last Sunday' and 73% 'the Sunday before last'. 16% averaged once every 2 or 3 weeks, 5% once a month and 9% less than once a month. The highest average attendance for the four churches was at Forest Hill, where 75% attended once or twice a week. In Crawley the figure was 60%. Perhaps this represents different norms in the four churches of what attendance should be. There were roughly similar proportions for all four churches of around 15% who attended once a month or less.

62% attended Communion once a month or more, 32% less than once a month or occasionally, and 6% never. Crawley and Upper Norwood showed very similar Communion attendance patterns and came very near to the overall average for attendance once a month or more frequently. There was a considerable difference between frequency of Communion at Byfleet (52% attended once a month) and Forest Hill (71%). The significance of this finding and the bearing of Communion attendance on ecumenical attitudes are dealt with later in the article. One would certainly expect a high level of attendance among Methodist members, as indeed one would expect this among all Nonconformists. As a recent book states: '. . . less than 30% of those calling themselves Nonconformist are entirely outside their churches' ministrations, compared with 40% of Anglicans and 20% of Roman Catholics.'[9]

Religious attitudes

In reply to the general question on unity, there were some interesting variations. Relevant data are shown in Table 5.

Table 5　RESPONDENTS' ATTITUDES TO UNITY IN GENERAL

	Byfleet	Crawley	Forest Hill	Upper Norwood	Total
Should aim for unity	61 %	54 %	46 %	58 %	55 %
Differences valuable	19	28	41	20	27
Difficult to say and no reply	20	18	13	22	18

The overall figure shows a majority of 55% who thought that Christians of different denominations should aim for unity and just over one-quarter who thought that differences were valuable. But the totals conceal an interesting distinction between Byfleet, which was most clearly positive towards church unity in general, and Forest Hill, where less than half the respondents were ecumenically-minded. Nor was this a result of indecision; indeed, Forest Hill respondents were more likely to have made up their minds than the members of any other church.

If we look at attitudes towards specific Christian groups a similar pattern emerges (see Table 6).

Table 6 RESPONDENTS' ATTITUDES TO
SPECIFIC GROUPS

Respondents replying that unity would be *good* or *very good* with:

	Byfleet	Crawley	Forest Hill	Upper Norwood	Total
Church of England	74	73	50	65	65
Baptists	68	77	54	56	64
Roman Catholics	17	22	2	10	13
Congregationalists	76	82	57	65	70
Presbyterians	74	72	50	57	63
Salvation Army	48	59	32	40	44
Quakers	32	44	18	24	29
Unitarians	16	18	9	6	12
Elim Pentecostal	17	14	6	6	11

The denomination which came first in terms of maximum preference overall and in each of the four churches was the Congregationalist. The Church of England was always among the top three preferences and the Baptists and Presbyterians were never far from the top of the list. After these four groups, however, there is a very distinct gap until we reach the Salvation Army (less than majority preference). A good way below the Salvation Army come the Quakers, and the least preferred groups were the Unitarians, Roman Catholics and Elim Pentecostal. But there is an unmistakable tendency for individual churches to have an ecumenical 'level' – i.e. to be consistently higher or lower than the average at every step in the order of preferences. If we average out the total percentages for each church to give an index of ecumenical inclination, we find that

Crawley heads the list (and, incidentally, had a much lower non-response for the more hypothetical cases than the other three churches). Byfleet is above average, Upper Norwood below average, and Forest Hill was even less prone to the pervasive ecumenicalism – it is worth noting that only 50% of its respondents favoured unity with the Church of England.

Some explanation of these findings is needed at this point, because it is becoming very apparent that Forest Hill, while conforming in many ways to the overall social and demographic pattern of the other four churches, and particularly the adjacent Upper Norwood, was obviously divergent on many of the religious attributes. In fact, the explanation supports the existence of some traditional 'religious factor' influencing observance and attitudes, since the church at Forest Hill had formerly been Primitive Methodist, part of the neo-sectarian wing of Methodism.[10] Primitive Methodism was furthest from the 'classical' Anglican-Tory tradition of Wesleyan Methodism and showed more sectarian characteristics. We should therefore expect a more negative attitude to ecumenicalism. The church at Forest Hill was an old-established church, which might account for the high attendance average. Communion attendance is likewise related to the old Primitive Methodist tradition: while Wesleyans held a more sacramental view of Communion – regarding the service as particularly holy – the Primitives regarded it much more as a matter of course and therefore attended more frequently. Their method of distributing the elements (stewards handed out Communion glasses and bread to the congregation in their seats) was still observed at Forest Hill. The attitudinal differences can best be described as 'Prim' rather than proper, and our finding is certainly in line with Bryan Wilson's statement that 'the laity [in Methodism] continues to nurture a sense of dissent' while the religious professionals strive for unity.[11]

We asked the same question as David Clark on what parts of the church service were most valuable.[12] Table 7 gives the results in the order in which they were listed in the questionnaire.

There were very few points of difference between the four churches, except that Upper Norwood respondents were more likely to see the whole service as valuable. The fact that Forest Hill respondents, despite their high Communion attendance, saw it as neither more nor less valuable than other churches suggests that their traditional views are linked more to the nature of the service than to its place

Table 7 PARTS OF THE SERVICE SEEN
AS MOST IMPORTANT

Percentage saying most valuable part was:

	Present survey	Clark's survey
Holy Communion	12%	11%
The whole service	37	34
Prayer	2	13
Sermon	11	19
Hymns	7	18
Bible-reading	1	5
Music	1	3
Alters according to need	27	7
No reply	3	—

in the overall structure of worship. The consistently high proportion
of respondents who thought the service altered according to need
supports the argument put forward by David Martin that the
denomination has a 'subjective approach to sacraments'[13] – what is
important is the state of mind of the recipient – 'need' – rather than
the objective dispensing of proprietary grace. But it does appear
from a comparison with Clark's figures that there is a difference
between Methodist membership and leadership. The latter were
rather more likely to have made a specific choice, particularly of
prayer, sermon or hymns.

Table 8 ATTITUDES TO VARIOUS ASPECTS OF WORSHIP

	Percentage describing aspects of worship as:				
	essential	not essential always helpful	occasionally helpful	no help at all	no reply
Psalm-chanting	1%	11%	31%	42%	15%
Hymn-singing	72	18	3	1	6
Free prayer by minister	65	20	6	1	8
Repeating Creed together	8	27	36	16	13
Kneeling for prayer	5	21	23	39	12
Minister wears special dress	8	21	11	47	13
Choir gowned	2	17	10	58	13
A cross on the altar or Communion table	39	31	7	11	12
Sermon	66	18	9	1	6

We then asked questions on aspects of Christian worship, using exactly the same scheme as David Clark but omitting the question on church notices.[14] Table 8 summarizes the results.

These results confirm David Clark's finding that hymn-singing is regarded as an essential part of worship by the highest proportion of Methodists, followed closely by the sermon and free prayer by the minister. A cross on the altar or Communion table came next in importance, but after this we had a different order from Clark's, in that repeating the Creed and the minister wearing special dress were equal fifth, followed by kneeling for prayer, choir gowned and last with only 1%, psalm-chanting. It is quite clear, on the other hand, that the overall Methodist membership is much more likely than the leadership to be outspoken on two particular issues and to dismiss them as being of no help at all: the two are psalm-chanting and kneeling for prayer. Differences between the four churches in our survey were very marginal.

In reply to the question, 'Is baptism necessary for a person to be a real Christian?' 30% said 'Yes', 60% said 'No' and 10% did not know or did not reply. The pattern was the same for each church. When asked, 'Do you think that a minister's ordination sets him apart fundamentally from other men?', 31% said 'Yes', 60% said 'No' and 9% did not know or did not answer, with again no variation between the four churches.

The next stage in the analysis was to compute various tabulations on the basis of the attitudinal data in order to measure the relationship between expressed opinion and other social, demographic and attitudinal characteristics. For the purposes of this article we will limit our discussion to the questions on unity in general and unity with the Church of England in particular (see above, p. 20) and the tabulations will be made on the total number of respondents.

A profile of attitudes to unity in general

The sex of respondents seemed to make little difference to attitudes to unity. 55% of men and 54% of women thought that Christians of different denominations should aim for unity. On the other hand, 31% of men as against 22% of women thought that differences were valuable, and 24% of women found it difficult to say or gave no reply. The only conclusion this leads to is that men are more likely to make their mind up one way or the other than women.

Marital status seemed to make very little difference to general unity attitudes, and there were no clearly observable trends as far as occupational, educational and political differences were concerned.

Interesting results appear when we tabulate age against attitude to unity (Table 9).

Table 9 THE INFLUENCE OF AGE ON ATTITUDES TO UNITY

Age group	Percentage in each age group holding attitude to unity:		
	should aim for unity	differences valuable	difficult to say and no reply
15–19	59·1 %	22·7 %	18·2 %
20–29	60·6	30·3	9·1
30–39	61·5	23·1	15·4
40–49	54·5	30·3	15·2
50–59	43·5	39·1	17·4
60–69	64·2	18·9	16·9
70 and over	38·1	26·2	35·7
Total	54·6	27·1	18·3
(Total number)	(179)	(89)	(60)

There is some evidence of a trailing-off of positive attitudes in the 40–49 age group, even more marked in the 50–59 age group and the 70+ age group. But the 60–69 age group contained the highest proportion of respondents who said the Christian churches should aim for unity. A satisfactory explanation of this finding cannot be given until we have analysed the data further, but some tentative explanations present themselves. It may well be that in this age group, which includes many recently-retired individuals, the need for wider social networks to give support in coping with increased leisure is strong enough for these networks to be sought in other Christian groups. In addition, many middle-class people move house when they retire, and may not be able to find a church of their previously attended denomination just round the corner.

On another point, there seems to be a syllogism in circulation (associated, we were told by one acquaintance, with 'ecumania') which can be summarized as:

Those who support ecumenicalism will become alienated if it fails to materialize.

The young are particularly enthusiastic towards ecumenicalism.

Therefore the Church will be alienating its future membership if it ignores ecumenicalism.

Our study suggests that we can give support to the minor premiss of this argument. It might even be strong enough to support the conclusion, but we have yet to see evidence in support of the major premiss.

It is when we begin to look at religious background and observance that some of the more interesting results emerge. First of all, we measured the effects of father's denomination, mother's denomination and baptismal denomination on the attitudes of respondents. The only two denominations in which there are enough people to make comparisons are the Church of England and the Methodist Church. The results are in Table 10.

Table 10 RELIGIOUS HISTORY AND
ATTITUDES TO UNITY

Attitude	Father's denomination		Mother's denomination		Baptismal denomination	
	Angli-can	Method-ist	Angli-can	Method-ist	Angli-can	Method-ist
In favour of unity	45·5%	58·3%	50·4%	56·1%	50·4%	58·9%
Differences valuable	37·1	26·7	31·1	28·0	32·2	26·6
Difficult to say and no reply	17·4	15·0	18·5	15·9	17·4	14·5

There is a clear and consistent, but not extreme, relationship between previous Anglican experience and a less positive attitude towards Christian unity, with the opposite tendency for lifelong Methodists. These figures lose some of their significance when it is noted that two-thirds of the English population identify themselves as Anglicans and two-thirds are actually baptized Anglicans.[15] But it does suggest the existence of a 'conversion syndrome': those who actively choose to join a group are more likely than others who have been socialized into it to want to preserve the distinctive existence of that group.

The same sort of relationship occurred when the number of respondents' relatives who were Methodist members was taken into account. As the number of relatives who were Methodists increased, so, very slightly, did positive attitudes to unity, so that out of 76 respondents who said almost all their relatives were Methodist members, 59% thought the Christian churches should aim for unity, while the percentage for the 83 who had no Methodist relatives was 52%. There was no difference in the proportion of respondents who said that differences were valuable, and a noticeably higher proportion of those with a few or no Methodist relatives found it difficult to decide.

There is apparently a strong positive correlation between average attendance and lack of enthusiasm for Christian unity. The figures are worth quoting in detail and are given in Table 11.

Table 11 AVERAGE ATTENDANCE AND ATTITUDE TO UNITY

Average attendance	In favour of unity	Differences valuable	Difficult to say and no reply
once or twice a week	48·0 %	32·8 %	19·2 %
once every 2/3 weeks	64·2	15·1	20·8
once a month	68·8	18·8	12·5
less than once a month	79·3	10·3	10·3

Those who were most involved in the religious activity of the Methodist Church were considerably less likely to favour unity than those who were least involved, though even among those who attended once or twice a week, 48% were in favour of unity.

A very similar effect was observed when Communion attendance was measured against attitude to unity, but it was less marked. 52% of those who attended Communion at least once a month as against 67% of those who never attended thought the churches should aim for unity. The corollary of this was also evident – frequent Communion attenders more often thought that differences were valuable.

Respondents who were members of any Methodist organization (guild, fellowship, youth club etc.) were also a good deal cooler towards the idea of unity than those who were not members. Similarly, a lower proportion of respondents who held office in Methodist organizations thought the churches should aim for unity than did the non-members. Table 12 contains the data.

This is interesting because it shows us which are the most likely of three possible hypotheses to explain the reaction of laity to the goal of religious unity. We have already quoted Bryan Wilson's

B

Table 12 THE ATTITUDES TO UNITY OF MEMBERS
AND NON-MEMBERS OF METHODIST ORGANIZATIONS

	In favour of unity	Differences valuable	Difficult to say and no reply
Non-members	65·4 %	18·7 %	15·9 %
Members	49·3	31·2	19·4
Office-holders	50·4	33·3	16·3

observation that religious professionals are more favourable towards unity than the laity in general (above, p. 28). From this we might imply two different hypotheses. The first could be labelled the 'hierarchical' hypothesis: if religious professionals are most involved in schemes of unity, those among the laity who come into contact most with the professionals as a result of their attendance at worship, their work in the church and their office-holding in various church organizations should share more attitudes with ministers than the laity at large. This would result in a more favourable than average attitude to unity. On the other hand there is the 'priesthood of all believers' hypothesis, which can also be inferred from the Wilson statement: those among the laity who are most active in the worship and organization of the church are likely to believe more strongly than most in the place of the laity when their status as the 'vox populi' and decision-making body in the Church comes into question. Thus we would expect them to represent to a heightened degree the tendencies present in the lay membership at large, and to be even cooler towards unity than average lay opinion. A similar result could be expected from the third hypothesis, which may be conveniently labelled the 'institutional' explanation. In this case we would expect that members of an organization who have a higher 'investment' than others in terms of attendance, activity and a particular status are likely to be more concerned than others to preserve the integral identity of that organization and hence to be less committed to schemes that would mean its erosion as a separate group. Our research in the four churches leads us to conclude that the second and third hypotheses are more convincing than the first. Interestingly, Currie[16] in several places describes the independence of Methodist leaders and the recurrent conflicts between lay officials and the professional ministry.

As might be expected, there was a consistently strong relationship between a positive attitude to unity in general and a positive attitude to each of the specific Christian groups listed. Of those who said unity with a particular church would be a 'very good thing', there were always around 80–90% who had previously expressed a positive attitude to unity in general. But an interesting tabulation can be produced by taking the group of respondents who said that differences between churches were valuable and then went on to say that unity with a particular church would be a very good thing. In this way we hoped to identify those churches which were perceived as being 'closest' to the Methodist Church. In fact there was a high degree of consistency, in that no more than one-fifth of those who said that differences were valuable ever said that unity with a particular church would be a very good thing. However, below this limit there is an interesting ranking of other Christian groups (Table 13).

Table 13 ECUMENICAL
'CLOSENESS'

Percentage of those who had said that differences were valuable who said it would be 'very good' to unite with:

Congregationalists	19%
Baptists	18
Presbyterians	15
Church of England ⎱ Salvation Army ⎰	10
Quakers	6
Elim Pentecostal ⎱ Roman Catholic Church ⎰ Unitarians	2

The Church of England may appear some way down the list because it is perceived in a different way from the others, as a real rather than a hypothetical possibility: in other words, you can be most charitable when you are least threatened. Equally, though, the explanation may be that the perceived difference of the Church of England *is* greater than that of the Nonconformist denominations and the Presbyterians.

Of those who said that Holy Communion was the most important part of the service, 62% thought the churches should aim for unity; of those who said the whole service was important the corresponding figure was 57%, and among those who said the definition of what was important altered according to need or who though the sermon was most important the figure was 53%. These were the only four parts of the service that contained sufficient numbers to make comparisons meaningful, and the differences are not very great, but the results make sense. Those who see Holy Communion as most important can obviously indicate several other churches in which this act of worship is seen as central, thus implying an element of shared observance. Those who saw the sermon or personal need as being most important may be characterized respectively as those who emphasize the 'Protestant' and the 'denominational' aspects of Methodism.

The relationships between the various aspects of worship and attitudes to unity were difficult to measure because they usually involved very small numbers under certain categories – for instance, only four people thought psalm-chanting was an essential aspect of worship. There were a few observable trends, however. Those who thought that repeating the Creed was essential were significantly more favourable towards unity – 76% of these respondents as against 48% of those who thought repeating the Creed was no help at all. 71% of those who thought kneeling essential wanted the churches to aim for unity compared with 48% who thought it was no help at all. 63% of those who thought baptism was necessary to make a person a real Christian were in favour of unity compared with 52% of those who did not, and there was a similar result (61% and 53%) for those who thought a minister's ordination set him apart fundamentally from other men. There is evidence here, albeit slight, of more formal and sacerdotal images of the Church among those who are in favour of unity.

A profile of attitudes to the Church of England

There were some changes of emphasis when we asked the question on unity with specific groups (see above, pp. 20 and 27). For the purposes of this article we are concentrating on attitudes to the Church of England because it represents a 'distinct possibility' rather than a hypothetical choice.

Women seemed to have a somewhat less favourable attitude to this church than men. Table 14 shows the differences.

The percentage of women who said unity with the Church of

England would be a very good thing was half that of the corresponding male percentage. This may largely represent differences in expression, because altogether 68% of men and 61% of women said it
would be a good or a very good thing, which shows a negligible
difference. Women were rather less likely to have made up their
minds.

Table 14 SEX OF RESPONDENTS HAVING
CERTAIN ATTITUDES TO THE CHURCH
OF ENGLAND

	Unity with the Church of England would be:				
	Very good	Good	Undecided/ no reply	Bad	Very bad
Men	43%	25%	24%	8%	—
Women	24	37	33	4	2%

Marital status made some difference to attitudes: 57% of single
respondents thought unity with the Church of England would be a
good or a very good thing while 68–69% of married and widowed
respondents thought so. It could be that single people tend to value
highly the 'fellowship' they find in the Methodist Church (the word
recurred constantly in respondents' comments on questionnaires)
and see less of this characteristic in the Church of England.

Two distinct age groups emerged, with once again a remarkable
upswing in positive attitudes in the 60–69 age group. Up to the age
of 49 around 75% of each age group thought that unity with the
Church of England would be a good thing or a very good thing.
Thereafter the figures were: 50–59, 54%; 60–69, 64% and 70 and
over, 38%. We are forced to conclude that in the 60–69 age group
there are special factors influencing attitudes.

Some differences were evident when we tabulated attitude to the
Church of England against occupation and education. Only 55%
of lower white-collar workers were in favour of unity compared with
72% of managers and employers. It could well be that for this group
Methodism provided higher-status internal roles than those provided
by the wider society and thus they were less prepared to unite with a
group which might minimize these roles. Other studies have shown
that religious groups can provide a 'substitute' status system to that
of the wider society.[17] Respondents educated at grammar schools
were rather more in favour of unity (69%) than were those educated

at elementary schools (55%), and university graduates were also much more in favour.

Interestingly, the percentage of respondents saying that unity with the Anglicans would be good or very good increased in direct relationship to the number of children in a family: those with one child included 62% who said unity with the Church of England would be good or very good; two children, 70%; three children, 70%, and four children, 84%. Taking this finding in conjunction with the occupational differences in attitude just mentioned, it seems that we could be dealing with 'the infertile clerk'.

Political allegiance seemed to make some difference to positive attitudes to Anglicanism. 74% of Conservatives said unity with the Church of England would be a good or a very good thing, 68% of Liberals and 64% of Labour supporters. There is considerable evidence to show that Conservative voters had correctly identified the predominant political colour of the Church of England.[18]

The relationship between parental/baptismal denomination and ecumenical attitude was similar to but much less marked than that described above (p. 32). The figures are given in Table 15.

Table 15 **RELIGIOUS HISTORY AND ATTITUDE TO THE CHURCH OF ENGLAND**

	Father's denomination		Mother's denomination		Baptismal denomination	
	Angli-can	Method-ist	Angli-can	Method-ist	Angli-can	Method-ist
Unity with Church of England good or very good	61	65	64	64	65	72

Those with Church of England backgrounds were rather less likely to favour unity with the Church of England; at the same time, the differences are not very large. There was hardly any difference at all between the attitudes of respondents who had most, some or none of their relatives Methodist members.

If we look at the average attendance and Communion attendance of those who said that unity with the Church of England would be good or very good, however, a very strong relationship is clearly visible (Table 16).

Table 16 AVERAGE AND COMMUNION ATTENDANCE AND ATTITUDE TO CHURCH OF ENGLAND

Those who said that unity with the Church of England would be a good or a very good thing		
Average attendance	%	Number
once or twice a week	61	139
once every two or three weeks	66	35
once a month	75	12
less than once a month	93	23
Communion attendance		
once a month or more	63	43
once a month	61	81
less than once a month but occasionally	71	75
never	78	14

We find here, as we found with attitudes to unity in general, that the most frequent attenders have the least positive attitudes towards unity with the Church of England. For all that, no category of attenders contained less than three-fifths who favoured unity.

As we might expect from the earlier data, members and office-holders in Methodist organizations were significantly less attracted to unity with the Church of England. 73% of non-members of Methodist organizations said unity would be good or very good; 62% of members said so, and only 56% of officeholders held this opinion.

We had thought that there might emerge two specific ecumenical 'directions', one towards the Church of England and one towards the Nonconformist denominations. In fact this was not the case because of those respondents who opted for unity with the Church of England the overwhelming majority were in favour of unity with the other denominations. Table 17 presents the evidence for this.

This suggests to us that the ecumenicalism of our Methodist respondents represented an all-round attitude of acceptance towards other denominations which excluded only those which had clearly distinct (i.e. sectarian or strongly ecclesiastical) attributes. This

Table 17 RESPONDENTS IN FAVOUR
OF UNITY WITH ANGLICANS
ALSO IN FAVOUR OF UNITY
WITH SPECIFIED DENOMINATIONS

Of the 214 respondents (65 % of the total sample)
who said unity with the Church of England
would be a good or a very good thing, the
percentage who had a similar attitude to unity
with the groups listed below were:

Congregationalists	85 %
Baptists	78
Presbyterians	78
Salvation Army	58
Quakers	38
Roman Catholic Church	19
Unitarians	17
Elim Pentecostal	15

indiscriminate recognition of other Christian bodies is hardly surprising and has been incorporated into the typological description of the denomination. Martin says:

'In the first place and perhaps pre-eminently the denomination rejects the whole concept of *Extra ecclesiam non salus* as defined in institutional terms.'[19]

However, although protagonists of unity between the Methodist Church and the Church of England can point to many shared features in the two churches, particularly those resulting from their common origin,[20] it would be necessary to specify that this close relationship with Anglicanism has never been as strong among the laity as it has among the ministry. While Wesley himself maintained a strong Anglican loyalty and tried to impose its observance on his members, it seems that he was drawing his recruits from an unchurched or at least disaffected segment of the population to whom Anglicanism had no special appeal. Our study bears this out because there is no evidence of a strong specific attachment to the Church of England.

We showed above (Table 8, pp. 29 and 30) that our respondents held a stongly Nonconformist view of what were essential aspects of worship and tended to be very unsympathetic towards those aspects of worship which can be seen as most typically Anglican. Some of these may, as David Clark notes,[21] be inessentials, but some of them represent central traditions in their respective churches.

The services of Morning and Evening Prayer in the Church of England, for example, are based on the monastic offices which are in turn based on the Psalms: similarly, Methodist theology has been transmitted to a great extent through hymns, particularly those of Charles Wesley. A formal credal statement is an important aspect of Anglican worship, just as free prayer is linked with the radical subjectivity of a Nonconformist denomination. The Communion service is perhaps the most crucial area of contact. We tabulated the attitudes of respondents towards the Church of England against their opinion of various aspects of worship (see Table 18) and it was at this point that we coined the phrase 'disembodied ecumenicalism' to describe our findings.

Table 18 ATTITUDE TO THE
CHURCH OF ENGLAND AND
ASPECTS OF WORSHIP

Of the 214 respondents who said that unity with the Church of England would be a good or a very good thing, the percentage who said that a particular aspect of worship was *essential* were:

Singing hymns	73 %
Free prayer by minister	66
Sermon	65
Cross on altar	43
Repeating Creed together	11
Minister wears special dress	9
Kneeling to pray	7
Choir gowned	3
Psalm-chanting	1

In several of these cases attitudes were so polarized that it was impossible to measure any relationship between the two sets of attitudes – for example, psalm-chanting – but in some cases attitudes to worship could be used as 'predictors' of attitudes to the Church of England. Repeating the Creed was a good example of a 'predictor': 24 of the 25 who thought it was an essential part of worship thought that unity with the Church of England would be a good or a very good thing; 74% of those who thought it non-essential but always helpful favoured unity; 63% of those who thought it occasionally helpful, and 56% of those who thought it no help at all had this attitude to the Church of England. There was a very similar positive relationship for attitudes to kneeling and a slight positive relationship for attitudes to the minister wearing special dress. No clear relationships emerged for the other aspects of worship.

Of those who thought baptism essential for a person to be a real Christian, 76% thought unity with the Church of England was a good or a very good thing, while for those who did not think it essential the corresponding figure was 63%. Thus of the 214 respondents who favoured unity with the Church of England 57% thought baptism was not essential.

Respondents' attitudes to the minister's ordination seem to have no effect on attitudes to the Church of England: around two-thirds of those who said they thought ordination set the minister apart from other men were in favour of Anglican unity, and so were a similar proportion of those who thought ordination did not set the minister apart.

Conclusion

The preceding article is based on frequency counts, cross tabulations and correlations, and the only additional analysis yet completed has been an attempt to let the responses speak for themselves by using a computer programme known as Algorithm for Interaction Detection (AID.).[22] Our concluding remarks will be based on the results of this analysis.

From our previous analysis we can state that 65% of our respondents thought that unity with the Church of England would be a good thing or a very good thing. We wanted to be able to state that a person with certain given characteristics would be in favour of unity, and already we have shown that certain characteristics are associated with particular attitudes towards other churches – for instance, age, attendance and parental denomination. The AID programme takes us one step further than this by isolating the variables which are most important using a reliable statistical technique. The results we obtained by our cross tabulations are largely confirmed by this method, as is shown in Table 19. Age is the most important variable in determining attitude to the Church of England. The data split into two significantly different groups: 54% of the people aged 50 and over were in favour of unity with the Anglicans while 74% of those under 50 gave a similar response.

Taking the younger age group first, the next most important variable is whether or not they attended church frequently: those who

Table 19 FACTORS INFLUENCING ATTITUDE TO THE CHURCH OF ENGLAND

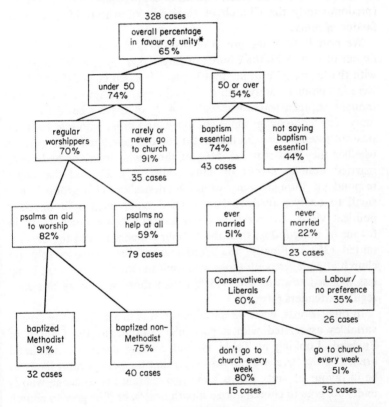

*Percentages refer to those stating that unity with the Church of England would be a good or a very good thing.

went to church infrequently (once a month or less) were more likely to accept unity with the Church of England. 70% of the regular attenders under 50 were in favour of unity compared with 91% of the infrequent attenders. Of those who went to church more than once a month, attitude to the Church of England was correlated with their attitude to chanting psalms. There was a group of 79 people who said that psalm-chanting was no help at all and 59% of these people were in favour of unity between the two churches.[23] 82% of those who found psalm-chanting at least some help stated that they were actively in favour of Anglican-Methodist unity. This last group finally split into two groups – those baptized as Methodists, of whom 91% wanted unity, and those baptized into other churches (predominantly the Church of England), of whom 75% were in favour of unity.

We now look at the group of over-50's, of whom 54% were in favour of unity with the Church of England. They split into a group with the 'churchy' attitude that baptism is essential – 74% of these were in favour of unity with the Anglicans – and into a group who thought baptism was not essential: 44% of these seemed to want unity. The 'churchy' group is left alone, and those who said baptism was not essential or who had not made up their mind next split on whether they had married. 51% of those who were, or had been, married were in favour of unity whilst only 22% of the single respondents thought unity would be desirable. This group is too small to analyse further. The married group next split on their political views, Conservatives and Liberals being much more in favour of unity (60%) than the Labour supporters and the uncommitted (35%). Finally, the Conservative/Liberal group split on church attendance, with those who went to church every week being less inclined towards unity (51%) than those who were not such regular attenders (80%).

In other words, what we have identified here are the really crucial variables associated with a particular attitude to the Church of England. Looking at Table 19 and reading down the left-hand branch of the 'tree' we can now state that the person most likely to be in favour of unity between the two churches is someone who is under 50, goes to church once a month or less, or if he goes to church more than once a month thinks that psalm-chanting is an aid to worship and was probably baptized a Methodist. Reading down the right-hand side, we can state that the person least likely to be in favour of Anglican-Methodist unity is 50 or over, does not think baptism is essential, is single, or if married is either a Labour supporter or is politically uncommitted. If he is a Conservative or Liberal then he is more likely to be a frequent attender. What we find most interesting is that of the eight 'splits' which emerged from the AID analysis, five related to aspects of religious belief or practice: this strongly supports the operation of the 'religious factor' in determining attitudes towards ecumenicalism.

NOTES

1. We wish to acknowledge the valuable advice of Dr David Martin in the preparation and analysis of this survey.

2. The criteria for membership of the Methodist Church are well-defined and ministers keep up-to-date lists. Members are sometimes called 'ticket-holders'.

3. See the article by Frank Pagden, 'An Analysis of the Effectiveness of Methodist Churches of Varying Sizes and Types in the Liverpool District', in *A Sociological Yearbook of Religion in Britain*, ed. David Martin, London: SCM Press, 1968, pp. 124–34.

4. An interesting reworking of this often-quoted feature of Methodist members is given by Alasdair MacIntyre, *Secularization and Moral Change*, London: Oxford University Press, 1967, pp. 48–49.

5. David B. Clark, *Survey of Anglicans and Methodists in Four Towns*, London: Epworth Press, 1965.

6. Margaret Stacey, *Tradition and Change: a Study of Banbury*, London: Oxford University Press, 1960.

7. Even so, it was on the basis of precisely this distinction that H. R. Niebuhr broke through Troeltsch's dichotomy and provided work for many hundreds of sociologists of religion. Religious typologizing is now a major sociological industry, rivalled only by the debate over the 'religious factor'.

8. See David Martin's article, 'The Denomination', *British Journal of Sociology*, 13.1, 1962, pp. 1–14, reprinted as an Appendix in *Pacifism*, London: Routledge and Kegan Paul, 1965, pp. 208–224, from which it is cited.

9. David Martin, *A Sociology of English Religion*, London: Heinemann and SCM Press, 1967, p. 40.

10. United with the original 'Wesleyan' Methodist Church and the United Methodist Church in 1932. A valuable account of the events leading to schism and later reunion in Methodism is given by Robert Currie in *Methodism Divided*, London: Faber and Faber, 1968.

11. Bryan R. Wilson, *Religion in Secular Society*, London: C. A. Watts, 1966, p. 165.

12. Clark, *op. cit.*, p. 37.

13. Martin, 'The Denomination', *op. cit.*, p. 217.

14. Clark, *op. cit.*, pp. 41–48.

15. Figures in David Martin, *A Sociology of English Religion*, pp. 36–37.

16. Currie, *Methodism Divided*, *passim*.

17. See, for example, the article by Bryan Wilson, 'An Analysis of Sect Development', *American Sociological Review* 24.1, 1959, pp. 3–15, and the article by Bryan R. Roberts, 'Protestant Groups and Coping with Urban Life in Guatemala City', *American Journal of Sociology* 73.6, 1968, pp. 753–770.

18. Several voting studies show a higher percentage of Tory voters in the Church of England than in other churches. For example, R. S. Milne and

H. C. Mackenzie, *Marginal Seat*, London: The Hansard Society for Parliamentary Government, 1958.

19. Martin, 'The Denomination', *op. cit.*, pp. 213–15.

20. An excellent example of this is the ecumenical study by Trevor Dearing, *Wesleyan and Tractarian Worship*, London: Epworth Press and SPCK, 1966.

21. Clark, *Survey of Anglicans and Methodists in Four Towns*, p. 97.

22. The purpose of the procedure used in this analysis is to attempt to explain one variable, in this case attitude to unity with the Church of England, in terms of several other variables such as sex, marital status and occupation. A searching process is employed which seeks to split the data into a set of sub-groups of the population (in a form similar to that of a family tree), such that each sub-group differs from every other sub-group as much as possible in terms of the variable being analysed and is a large enough sub-group to matter. See, for example, John A. Ross and Sook Bang, 'The AID Computer Programme, Used to Predict Adoption of Family Planning in Koyang', *Population Studies* 20.1, 1966, pp. 61–75.

23. We have not looked further at this group which is typically 'Free Church' in attitude.

2 Institutional Persistence and Ecumenicalism in Northern Methodism

Bryan Turner

IT IS a paradoxical fact that, amongst the many problems which beset a social institution, its own membership constitutes a major organizational obstacle to success. Consequently, it is a basic assumption of organizational theory that sociological analysis must be at least two-directional, in the sense that theory attempts to conceptualize the impact of the internal compliance or resistance of persons on the external achievement of goals. Whilst this assumption would appear to be a necessary one, much contemporary analysis of ecumenicalism is entirely one-sided in so far as it concentrates exclusively on religious co-operation at national levels between leaders of the churches without examining the sort of strains this produces inside the churches. In this research report, data gathered by a survey of a Methodist district will be drawn upon to show that, whilst amalgamation may be a solution to organizational decline, it raises problems of authority and autonomy of sub-units within an organization. My contention is that the apparent consensus between church leaders over the desirability of church unity creates within churches potentially disruptive areas of conflict.

In order to give my data focus, my argument will hinge on themes and assumptions derived from a recent comprehensive 'sociological comment' on British religion.[1] In common with A. MacIntyre, A. Eister and others, Bryan Wilson shares the view that industrialization, urbanization and the concomitant differentiation of social institutions have made the churches more and more socially marginal. Furthermore, science, humanistic disciplines, and alternative secular ideologies have not only thrown doubt on religious assumptions, they have drastically undermined them. To quote from Alasdair MacIntyre, 'They [the churches] have as social institutions lost their importance for the community at large. They no longer provide any focus for the variety of communal activities. Hence religion itself has changed and has become a matter of private life and individual choice and taste, rather than the fabric of the social order.'[2] Related to this change in the socio-cultural backcloth of secularization is the hypothesis that Nonconformist institutions, in particular, have experienced a common shift from sectarianism to denominationalism, which is itself defined as a loss of pristine values. The contemporary response of the churches, it is claimed, to institutional marginality and the decline of faith is ecumenicalism. The preparedness to submerge denominational differences is made possible on two grounds. Firstly, the churches are weak and it is believed, therefore, that amalgamation will bring strength through efficiency. Secondly, the theological differences which separated the churches in the past have either been whittled away in the process of denominationalization, or are no longer perceived as significant, or can be by-passed. The general hypothesis of ecumenicalism is simply 'that organizations amalgamate when they are weak rather than when they are strong, since alliance means compromise and amendment of commitment'.[3] However, ecumenicalism is, in the long run, an inadequate solution for institutional decline, since it represents a turning of the church in on itself and away from society.

Whilst this is the major content of Bryan Wilson's position on this issue, there are three important 'specifications' of this general ecumenical hypothesis. Firstly, it is recognized that, despite ecumenical negotiations at the top level, local churches are often resistant to any form of change. 'There is,' Bryan Wilson claims, 'a general social phenomenon of institutional persistence, which is perhaps especially evident in the case of religious institutions, which, possibly because they are ultimate repositories of strong emotional commitment, however latent and traditional that commitment has become, manifest an especial durability.'[4] Whilst paper amalgamations can be achieved at Conference level, amalgamation at society level is frequently precluded by local tradition and conservativism. The second specification is that the ecumenical movement is clergy-dominated. For the Methodist minister, ecumenicalism provides a means by which he may finally equalize his social status with that of his Anglican counterpart. On the other hand the 'laity, who have less vested interest in this level of operation of their religious denomination, have shown themselves less enthusiastic about it'.[5] The final specification of the hypothesis of ecumenical religion, which we have been examining, is the recognition that, although religion may come to fulfil important social functions in the future, these functions will be supplied not by 'the religion which accepts the values of the new institutionalism, the religion of ecumenism, but the religion of the sects'.[6]

In this paper, from research into Methodism, an analysis of intra-organizational dilemmas, emerging from ecumenicalism, will be examined in terms of institutional persistence, laity and clergy dissensus and the resulting growth of splinter groups in Methodism, which foster a return to the earlier values of a pre-denominational Methodism. The research consists of a survey of members of the Methodist Church in one Methodist district with a membership of 23,237 persons in 288 societies. The name of this district is withheld from this report, so that the guarantee of anonymity may not be jeopardized. The sample was taken by clustering the societies into three size categories and then within each cluster taking a random sample of 19 societies, giving 57 in all. From the societies in each cluster, a disproportionate sampling fraction was employed to obtain 200 persons from each size category of church, giving an overall sample of 600 persons. A 50% sample of Methodist ministers was taken from the District in order to make lay–minister comparisons. 84% of the laity responded to the questionnaire and 98% of the ministers did so. The questionnaire is an adaptation of items on religious commitment, which has been developed by C. Y. Glock and R. Stark in their American research.[7]

In the early stages of the pilot study, it became evident that, despite attempts by local clergy to sponsor inter-church co-operation, the growth of local ecumenism is a slow, painful process. An attempt was made to classify the type of relation existing between local Anglican and Methodist churches, by size of Methodist church. No claim is made for the theoretical power of this classification, rather the table is of descriptive interest only.

If we combine the two middle rows of the matrix, we find that in

SIZE OF CHURCH

Type of Relation	Large	Medium	Small	Total
Hostile	4	5	1	10
No linkage	8	3	13	24
Superficial linkage	3	7	2	12
Extensive linkage	4	4	3	11
Total (societies)	19	19	19	57

36 of the 57 societies in the sample, there were no, or only superficial, co-operative relations between Methodist and Anglican churches in the district. 'No relationship' meant that there was no interchange of pulpits and no use made of interdenominational talks. In particular, these churches did not avail themselves of facilities offered by the 'People Next Door' movement. Church relations were classified as 'superficial' where there was an annual interchange of church premises.'Hostile' relations were situations in which neither minister was on speaking terms and where both denominational groups viewed each other with suspicion or antagonism. Extensive co-operation existed between Anglicans and Methodists in 11 churches, in which both ministers had organized a joint policy for both denominations.

Geographical and historical factors play an important part in determining no or superficial linkage between denominations. The small Methodist church is predominantly in rural areas where there is no Anglican church with which to establish relations, so that in these areas there is no content to the ecumenical process. Hostile relations were produced almost invariably by differences of opinion, or worse, between the local Anglican and Methodist minister. Frequently, Methodist ministers felt that the local Anglican clergyman was 'too autocratic' and local Anglicans 'too arrogant'. In one instance, ill-feeling was caused by the fact that the local Anglican clergyman refused to allow the children of Methodists into his Sunday School. To give one final example, one local Anglican clergyman was asked to give a talk on ecumenicalism to a Methodist society. After some reluctance, he gave a talk in which he claimed that, since Wesley himself was an Anglican, there was no such thing as a 'Methodist' and therefore the Anglican-Methodist conversations were a waste of time. These conflicts are partially explained by personality differences and by the frustrations of inferior or ambiguous status, but also by the fact that most high Anglican clergy wanted to keep the way open to future co-operation with the Catholic Church and were fearful lest close ties with Methodism would frustrate this future goal. Despite geographical problems and lay apathy, many Methodist ministers achieved close co-operation with Anglicans, in cases where leadership was exercised by both sides. However, most churches found that they had difficulty enough finding leaders for internal study and devotional groups without having to strain their resources for ecumenical groups.

The picture which emerged from the pilot study with the ministers was one in which resourceful Methodist ministers struggled to create ecumenicalism against an apathetic laity and a hostile Anglican clergy. This picture is considerably modified in the data from the questionnaires sent to Methodist laity and ministers. Responses to ecumenical items in the questionnaire suggest that not only are Methodist laity not persuaded of the desirability of Anglican-Methodist unity, but they are positively against it. Furthermore, whilst the ministers were comparatively favourable towards Anglican-Methodist unity, 36% of them thought it would do nothing to help the church cope with its present difficulties. The lay rejection of ecumenicalism will be considered first, before attention is turned to the lay/clergy dissensus.

Interviews with lay members during the pilot study indicated that Methodists would accept a union with Anglicanism which would not entail a total loss of identity for Methodism. The demand for 'unity, not uniformity' in practical terms implies a demand for denominational co-operation which is less than organic union. The fear of loss of autonomy was present in the response to the questionnaire. When asked how they felt about the proposed unity with Anglicanism, most said that complete union would involve Methodism being 'swallowed up in Anglicanism'. They were also asked to indicate which of nine denominations they would join, consider joining or not join, if, for some reason, they could no longer continue in the Methodist Church. The typical group of denominations chosen as an alternative to Methodist membership was composed of Presbyterian, Congregational and Baptist churches. The two most strongly rejected alternatives were Roman Catholicism and Jehovah's Witnesses. Anglicanism was an ambiguous choice. Some would consider it and others rejected it, but the Anglican Church came well below the choice for a Nonconformist denomination. Whilst they were willing to make hypothetical choices, the general consensus was that they 'wanted to stay as they were'. An instructive metaphor for the sort of church co-operation which they would tolerate came from a woman respondent who said, 'The Church is like a market. We all have our own stalls, but there's no need to be all under the same canvas.' Finally, Methodists were asked to rank eight denominations, religions and philosophies in order of similarity with Methodism. The resulting scale, although not intensively analysed as yet, was: Congregational, Presbyterian and Baptists as most

similar, Anglican in the middle and to the far end of the similarity
scale Catholic, Jew, Mohammedan and atheist. On this and other
questions relating to Catholicism, great hostility and bigotry were
shown to be common attitudes towards the Roman Catholic Church.
Quite a number of respondents went so far as to say that, as Catholicism was not a religion, but more like a dictatorship, it could in no
way be similar to Methodism. Of the more extreme rejections of
ecumenism as 'the road to Rome', the following extract from a letter
received from a male respondent is not untypical:

> Ministers have no mandate in the matter of church takeover bids. The people
> should decide this matter. Those ministers who are making themselves lap-
> dogs to Rome should be censured, they are traitors to Methodism. There
> should be no link up by Methodists with the Church of England, there's a
> difference between chalk and cheese.

The strong adherence to Nonconformist tradition and a rampant,
almost nineteenth-century, bigotry against Roman Catholicism on
the part of many laity raises acute problems for future ecumenical
negotiations. Firstly, Methodists fear that a close union with
Anglicanism would commit them to a communion which has close
ties with the Roman Church. Secondly, if a Methodist-Anglican
union takes place, it will make Anglican-Catholic negotiations
extremely difficult. These difficulties make the likelihood of large
sections of Methodists splintering away from the present Methodist
Church highly probable. Before examining the lay/minister dissensus
and the emergence of anti-ecumenical groups within Methodism,
the factors making for Methodist persistence will be briefly noted.

In so far as religious institutions approximate more to communities than to religious audiences, they are more resistant to change.
Strong communal and family ties with the local church seem characteristic of this reasearch district and partially explain the resistance
both to closure and to amalgamation, whether with other Methodist
societies or the Anglican church. The small size of Methodist
societies fosters much of the typical face-to-face relations found in
Methodism. One third of the societies in the district have a membership of under 34 persons, two thirds under 85, and the average size
of church was 81, which compares with a national average size of
society in 1963 of 64.[8] Associated with size of society is the fact that
Methodism is still well represented, although not necessarily strong,
in rural areas. In 1958, a Conference commission reported that
'Between one third and one half of the total membership of our

church lives in rural circuits'.[9] The rural isolation of large sections of the Methodist church engenders strong local attachments to the chapel, especially where it holds a monopoly of religious and social services.

Another important factor in this religious solidarity centres on kinship and friendship relations. When asked where they had found most of their present friends, respondents most frequently replied, 'in church.' In small churches especially, it was common for a respondent to have all his friends in one congregation. Kinship ties were equally strong. The typical Methodist has Methodist parents, has married a Methodist and has Methodist children. Even among graduates from university and training colleges, the Methodist Societies in higher education had functioned as adequate marriage markets. It is ironic to note that, whilst Methodists thought it unfair for Catholics to insist that children of mixed marriages be brought up as Catholics, exactly the same processes of group endogamy operate *de facto* in Methodism. In a sample of 600 Methodists, one case of a Catholic-Methodist marriage had occurred and a mere handful of Anglican ones. Where inter-denominational marriage occurs, it is normally between Congregationalists and Methodists.

Institutional persistence based on local solidarity is further bolstered by the middle age of the members and by the fact that the majority of Methodists are female. This is especially characteristic of the small churches, where 70% were women. On all items in this survey, women and the older members were consistently more conservative in their attitudes than the young and the male members of the congregation. To summarize this section, ruralism, size of society, kinship, sex and age function to reinforce the primary group qualities of the Methodist church and, as 'ultimate repositories of strong emotional commitment', they prove very resistant to change in the form of ecumenicalism and organizational rationalizations, such as the closure of redundant churches.

Turning to the issue of a lay/clergy split over ecumenism, where the laity were opposed to an Anglican-Methodist union of a total nature, the Methodist ministers were far more favourable to such a merger. It ought to be kept in mind that with such a small group of ministers in the sample, the figures quoted are of descriptive interest only. When asked about their attitudes towards union, 47% of the ministers said it was wholly desirable and would help the church to fulfil its mission in society, 36% thought it was desirable but would do little to solve the church's problems and 18% opposed union either totally or at least on the present basis. Interestingly, the ministers saw Methodism as far closer to the Anglican tradition than to the Nonconformist tradition. Where the laity ranked Presbyterianism as closest to Methodism, the ministers placed Anglicanism as most similar. 78% thought that 'it was a pity the Methodists had to leave the Anglican Church' and 20% disagreed with the statement. The major point of agreement between ministers and laity over ecumenism came with their mutual rejection of Roman Catholicism.

Whilst the Methodist minister has a favourable attitude towards union with Anglicanism, his organizational role means that an ecumenical posture is shot through with difficulties. In order to pinpoint the origins of this dilemma, it will be necessary to examine the tradition of high and low Methodism.[10] Historically, Methodism has suffered from a decentralization/centralization organizational conflict, which was produced by the existence within Methodism of two contradictory institutional polities, namely high and low Methodism. High Methodism is strictly speaking Wesleyanism, which adheres to a polity in which the Conference is the supreme authority in the denomination and is represented at the lowest level by the itinerant minister. Low Methodism was opposed to 'connexionalism' since in its polity the local society, represented by the class leader and local preacher, is the focus of authority. This institutional conflict lay behind all the denominational splits in nineteenth-century Methodism, was influential in the dissension prior to the 1932 union and, in the contemporary situation, exerts a significant ideological role in the heart-searching over Anglican-Methodist unity. Whilst low Methodism has declined, it is precisely in terms of low Methodist tradition that all the dissentient objections against union are couched. The decline of low Methodism can be seen in terms of the diminution of influence of lay roles and the local church as against the enhancement of the minister's organizational status and the growth of centralization. The number of fully accredited preachers has dropped from 34,948 in 1934 to 21,217 in 1964, which, in terms of local preachers as a percentage of membership, is a fall from 4·1% to 2·9%. The class system has been transformed into a 'ticket system', that is, a situation in which members are organized into classes which never or rarely meet. Of the 57 churches in my sample only two had classes which met regularly. Whilst the social basis of low Methodism has shrunk, the Methodist minister is, so to speak, ideologically circumscribed by these lay role components. According to the Deed of Union of the Methodist Church, ministers 'hold no priesthood differing in kind from that which is common to the Lord's people' and, furthermore, 'For the sake of Church Order and not because of any priestly virtue inherent in the office, the Ministers of the Methodist Church are set apart by ordination to the Ministry.' Even where the social basis of lay involvement has disappeared, its ideological significance is paramount, since it was precisely on low Methodist principles that the Dissentient Methodists based their criticism of union.

The problematic nature of lay/minister relations in Methodism cannot be isolated from the relationship between ministers and Anglican clergy. These role ambiguities would suggest that from the Methodist minister's point of view the acceptance of an Anglican view of the priesthood would offer at least one solution to these problems. Bryan Wilson's interpretation of this is:

> There is abundant evidence of the way in which the ministers of dissenting or free denominations experience some sense of flattery to be approached on practically equal terms by the clerics of more orthodox denominations.[11]

Against this interpretation, it is necessary to keep in mind the fact that when two weak organizations seek amalgamation, the stronger of the two amalgamating institutions will be able to enforce its view of institutional culture and thereby demand more compromise from the weaker organization. In particular, Anglican adherence to historic episcopacy would virtually wipe out the validity of the Methodist ministry. The dissentient ministers were acutely aware of this fact and commented that the Service of Reconciliation, specifically the laying on of hands, 'casts an intolerable (though certainly unintended) slur on Methodist ordinations and ministries in the past'.

Whilst ecumenicalism may be a pseudo-solution to organizational decline, it raises other problems which intensify the rate of organizational collapse. In particular, ecumenicalism is a threat to the autonomy of Methodist societies and to the professional status of the Methodist minister. In this situation, at least two strategies, withdrawal from and reconstitution of the organization, are being mobilized by two major dissentient groups, the Voice of Methodism and the national Liaison Committee.[12] The Voice of Methodism Association (VMA) has four objectives: to reject the proposals of Methodist-Anglican unity, to work for a Methodist revival, to establish stronger links with other Nonconformist organizations and 'to follow humbly the leading of the holy Spirit believing that the only true unity will be such as Christ wills'.[13] In plain terms, the object of the VMA is to re-vamp a declining low Methodism, since its specific fears relate to the declining role of the components of low Methodism. In a letter to a local paper, one Methodist minister, who was rejecting the present basis of union, enumerated the following fears he had for the present state of Methodism: the growing centralization of power at the expense of the local church, the gradual elimination of laymen, the frequent re-election of salaried officials and District chairmen after their normal period of office, the introduction of clerical uniforms, the ritualization of the communion service, the cooling-off in Methodist relations with other free churches and the increasing deference paid by ministers to 'their more exalted brethren'. The alienation of dissentient Methodists from the bureaucratization of contemporary Methodism is indicated by the annoyance felt towards 'circuit officials'. The VMA recommends that its local study groups

> must be free from interference by connexional or circuit officials: so we suggest that groups should not meet on Trust premises except where ministers are taking a leading part.[14]

Dissentient Methodists have thus mobilized a splinter organization within Methodism which, if union occurs, wants to withdraw from the uniting churches, but, whether the amalgamation occurs or not, it seeks a reconstitution of Methodism on traditional lines.

In conclusion, it has been argued that institutional persistence, the lay rejection of ecumenicalism and the ambiguities of the Methodist minister's role make union with Anglicanism of an organic nature highly problematic. Moreover, the analysis of social relations within Methodism suggests that the growth of inter-organizational links will not take the form of a British 'melting pot' of Nonconformist/Anglican/Catholic, in which all three have an interchangeable status. Rather we can expect to find religious institutions clustering into evangelical, ecumenical and Catholic denominations, with little or no linkage between the three groups.

NOTES

1. B. R. Wilson, *Religion in Secular Society*, London: Watts, 1966.
2. A. MacIntyre, 'Secularisation', *The Listener*, 15 February 1968 (Vol. 79, No. 2029).

3. Wilson, *op. cit.*, p. 126.
4. Wilson, *op. cit.*, p. 29.
5. Wilson, *op. cit.*, p. 230.
6. Wilson, *op. cit.*, p. 233.
7. The original American questionnaire has appeared in C. Y. Glock and R. Stark, *Christian Beliefs and Anti-Semitism*, New York: Harper and Row, 1966.
8. Quoted by F. Pagden, 'An Analysis of the Effectiveness of Methodist Churches of Varying Types and Sizes in the Liverpool District', *A Sociological Yearbook of Religion in Britain*, 1968, p. 126.
9. Commission on Rural Methodism from the *Agenda of the Representative Session of the Conference*, Newcastle, 1958.
10. For a discussion of high and low Methodism, John Kent, *The Age of Disunity*, London: Epworth Press, 1966, ch. 2, is most instructive.
11. Wilson, *op. cit.*, p. 130.
12. A theoretical account of organizational strategies for coping with threats to functional autonomy is to be found in A. W. Goulder, 'Reciprocity and Autonomy in Functional Theory', in L. Gross (ed.), *Symposium on Sociological Theory*, Evanston: Row, Peterson, 1958.
13. *The Declaration and Aims of the Voice of Methodism Association* (as set forth by the inaugural conference of the Association in 1963), London: VMA.
14. *Suggested Syllabus of Group Studies*, London: VMA.

3 Conflict in Minister / Lay Relations

Kenneth C. Dempsey

Introduction

THIS paper is an account of progress and findings to date in a continuing study of tension and conflict in minister/lay relations in an Australian Methodist Church.

Most of the data for the analysis has emerged from a microstudy[1] of minister/lay interaction in a particular rural congregation, namely Barool[2] in Northern New South Wales. Supportive data was gathered during two visits to Ministers' Seminars in Victoria, from conversations with many ministers and leading laymen, and from a variety of written reports. As a result I have reason to believe that the pattern of relationships found in Barool is widespread, and that emerging findings,[3] while not a basis for unqualified generalization, have some relevance beyond their immediate context.

The general purpose of the paper is to provide the reader with some insight into the nature of the research which was undertaken, the initial conception of the research plan, and the way in which subsequent investigations led the writer into interests and problems not originally contemplated.

It is intended also to indicate in broad outline the main conclusions arrived at so far, which may serve to initiate further investigations in the same field.

Emergence of the Central Problem

I began the investigation with no more definite aim than the desire to understand something of what was going on in a particular local church.

Initially, therefore, the study of minister/lay relations was approached as only one among many areas of interaction worthy of investigation. It was soon apparent, however, that the nature of minister/lay relations was the fulcrum upon which all else seemed to turn. Conversations and interviews with laymen inevitably moved to a discussion of the positive and negative qualities of each minister in a long succession of ministers, more often than not highlighting the periods of tension in the church's history and citing ministers alleged to be responsible for that tension.

From the layman's point of view there was a one for one relation between the quality of the minister and the organizational success of the church. Good congregations, active organizations, and a healthy balance sheet were the natural outcomes of a 'good' ministry. Conversely, poor congregations, inactive organizations and financial difficulties could invariably be attributed to a 'poor' ministry. Statements such as the following were commonplace:

> If the minister does his job the people come to church and we can pay our way.

> If these young ministers would only visit the people like the ministers did when I was a boy we could have a packed church and no financial worries.

It was also obvious from details of incidents and disagreements recounted by Barool laymen that in at least some cases there was a discrepancy between ministers' own role descriptions and the way in which the laymen defined the minister's role. Ministers and laymen had also disagreed over the content of the laymen's role, especially over the laymen's assumption that it was their right to instruct the minister in his duties and responsibilities. To the present writer laymen repeatedly expressed their position in this way:

> If I employ a man on my property I expect to tell him what to do, and to see to it that he does it. He accepts that this is proper and correct because I am paying him for his services. It should be no different with the minister. He'd be out of a job if we didn't pay him and provide him with a home. Therefore we should be able to tell him what he does rather than letting him do what he likes.

Conversations with various ministers prior to this investigation together with first-hand experience of a number of congregations made it abundantly clear that the discrepancy in mutual role definitions, revealed in the early stages of the investigation, were not peculiar to Barool. In a number of instances in both Barool and elsewhere, this disparity in mutual role definition was paralleled by either open conflict or a severing of relationships.

The disparity in role definition provided one focus for the study. At this stage I considered taking it as the main focus, dispensing altogether with the micro-study of Barool and, by using a random sample of laymen and ministers, comparing and contrasting their respective role definitions. Religious attitudes, beliefs and values would have provided additional related indices. Further, both the lay and ministerial sections of the sample could have been classified and re-classified according to such standard categories as education, occupation, class, degree of church participation and the relation between these and the various role definitions and prescriptions shown. Finally degree of divergence in role definitions between ministers and laymen could have been correlated with the degree of conflict occurring.[4]

Such an approach would have yielded a body of substantive information in an area where our present knowledge is negligible and would have had the added advantage of being theoretically neatly structured and technically easily manageable.

Despite its advantages, I rejected this and other closely related approaches for a number of reasons. First, from the beginning I viewed this investigation as an exploratory study. Our systematic knowledge of minister/lay relationships in this country, as of almost any aspect of the sociology of religion in Australia, is negligible. I felt, therefore, that an approach which in large part predetermined findings was to be avoided. In short, a study of a random sample of ministers and laymen would lessen the chances of the study being significant, in the sense of yielding unexpected information and of uncovering problems worthy of fuller investigation. Secondly, the preliminary investigation had convinced me that norm disparity was not in itself sufficient explanation for all of the conflict occurring between ministers and laymen in Barool. As Marx had long ago pointed out, internal conflict arises from the structure of the group itself.

It was obvious in this instance that both formal and informal features of the structure of the local congregation were related to tensions and conflict between ministers and laity. The problem, therefore, was to gain insight into these features of the group's structure. This was achieved in part, through the use of documentary evidence and the interviewing of participants. However, to delineate the *subtleties* of the informal structure and to unravel its complex relationships with the formal structure, I had to adopt the role of participant observer. It was in these circumstances that a micro-study, in which a critical method was participant observation, assumed such importance. Whilst such a micro-study does not yield statistically significant generalizations, and is often theoretically and methodologically untidy, in this instance its advantages over possible alternative approaches more than compensated for these 'shortcomings'. Specifically it allowed the observation of the actual interactions of participants in their social setting. Further, it permitted the 'totality' of the setting to be taken into account. Hence, although the study focused on a specific set of interactions within the local congregation, it never lost sight of other interrelationships outside of minister/lay relationships. Again, it facilitated the analysis of the association between a group's historical development and its present structure and culture. Above all, it permitted the investigator to plot in detail both the group's informal and formal structures, and the relationship of these to social behaviour and the group's beliefs and norms.[5]

At the risk of labouring the point, and even of some overstatement, I want to emphasize again the great importance of participation in the life of the church, as opposed to mere observation, for the satisfactory execution of an investigation of this kind. Not only had access to meetings to be gained, but once gained, it involved behaving in these and and informal gatherings as an ordinary interested member.[6] In this way it was possible to be present when important decisions were made and to observe the patterns of interaction, political alignments, gossip and urging that inevitably accompanied such decision-making. Through the assumption of such a role, I obtained the confidence and co-operation of the church's politically significant[7] members without which a study of any depth would have been impossible. So understood, participant observation meant living in the community in order to gain that acceptance which would legitimize my participation in church affairs and keep me in touch with day to day gossip, rumour, comment and behaviour, both inside and outside the church. The value of residence for this kind of study was confirmed after leaving Barool. Although members welcomed me readily enough on my return visits to church functions, non-residence reduced my role to that of mere observer and attracted unwanted attention to my peculiar purpose for being present.

Considerations such as these also led me to reject the idea of undertaking a comparative study of minister/lay relations of all the churches of the town. It simply was not possible to be accepted as a member of each church in a society where people normally belong to one.

Political Sub-structures within the Congregation

Because it was plain that the congregation was not a monolithic structure, the problem was to delineate the congregational sub-structures that *were* significant for minister/lay co-operation and conflict. Were there people who consistently opposed a particular minister or a number of ministers? If so, which people were these? Again, did support for the minister come consistently from any one quarter? If the answer was in the affirmative, which quarter was this? Was opposition more likely to lead to serious conflict if it came from a particular type of member or a particular sub-group or sub-groups of the congregation?

How far does knowledge of the formal and informal system enable us to answer these questions? In terms of the formal system, the questions can be only partly answered. There was *some* connection between the formal structure of the congregation and the patterns of conflict and co-operation. Thus, for example, it could be shown that conflict was more likely to occur between the minister and an appointed lay leader, or lay leaders, than between a minister and an ordinary member. Further, it appeared that any disagreement or conflict was more likely to have serious consequences if it was with an appointed lay leader rather than with an ordinary member. But an analysis in terms of the formal structure alone still left many questions unanswered. For example, conflict seems to be more likely with some leaders than with others; which were these? Why did the opposition of some appointed leaders never trouble the minister, and yet the opposition of some ordinary members lead to serious conflict?

Two things were readily evident: first, people varied in terms of their political significance, and second this variation did not neatly parallel the church's formal structure. This being the case, I had to develop a typology which would facilitate the accomplishing of my aim of classifying members according to their political significance. Political significance was assessed by (1) observing decision-making processes, (2) analysing informal cliques, (3) making case studies of critical incidents in the life of the church in recent years, and (4) obtaining parishioners' assessments of their fellow parishioners' place in the church's life, e.g., 'Which persons in the church carry most weight?' Members of the congregation were placed at a number of points along a continuum, ranging from the politically insignificant to the politically powerful. This analysis produced the following categories: Key Leaders, Secondary Leaders, Formers of Opinion, and the Politically Insignificant.[8]

On the continuum, the Key Leaders are those members who have most ability to influence the course of events. No important change can be made without their support. At the other end of the continuum, the Politically Insignificant[9] are those whose support or opposition is dispensable. Between these extremes are located first, the Secondary Leaders, who are essentially conservative and non-innovators, but whose votes and informal influence are valued by the Key Leaders. Secondly, the Formers of Opinion, some of whom are non-attending members of official meetings who yet exercise a degree of political influence by acting as channels of communication, as initiators of dissent or support, as interpreters of decisions in which they have not always participated, and as moulders of a general consensus. Such activities are not the prerogative of this group alone but are shared by the Key and Secondary Leaders, as a subsidiary aspect of their role.

Membership of all political categories appears to be closely related to such variables as occupation, general standing in the community, length of residence in the area, extent of kinship network and type of family connexions. However, the qualifications for leadership are both personal and social, embracing such qualities as personal integrity, long and faithful tenure of office, clarity of verbal expression, long-standing residence in the district and economic independence. Possession of an extensive kinship network from which supportive secondary leadership can be drawn is an advantage. In essence a Key Leader is one who (1) clearly and forcefully represents the congregation's viewpoint *vis-à-vis* that of the minister, (2) represents with equal vigour the minister's and congregation's viewpoint *vis-à-vis* other local groups, and (3) rallies lay support for, or resistance to, ministerially initiated innovation. When the minister is deviating extensively and consistently from the parishioner's conceptualization of his job, the Key Leader is one who crystallizes subdued murmuring into explicit and coherent opposition. In other words, he will often force a public show-down.

Sources of Minister/Lay Conflict

An essential problem was getting enough data on minister/lay conflict to gain an adequate understanding of its nature and the diverse factors contributing to it.

The most readily available information was that gained from direct participant-observation in the Barool Methodist Church, and structured and unstructured interviews of members and ministers during a two-year period in which there was a succession of four ministers. Supplementary contemporary data on other Methodist congregations were gained from informal contacts with ministers and laymen elsewhere in New South Wales and in Victoria. However, without adequate knowledge of the formal and informal structures from which it derived, it was of limited usefulness. It was the historical study of changes in the Barool Church itself which was most helpful in clarifying the problems implicit in the data collected by participant observation. By degrees I built up a reasonably complete picture of the formal and informal structure of the church by drawing on the reminiscences of elderly and long-standing members, previous ministers (or their relatives) and by examining church records and newspaper reports. This research also yielded an historical outline of the norms and social characteristics of ministers and laymen. It was thus possible to analyse instances of conflict or co-operation against a reconstructed picture of the normative and social framework. Furthermore, historical research exposed the fact (1) that conflict had occurred, and (2) that it had occurred at an increasingly rapid rate during the twentieth century. This was especially so in the period 1945–66 when a growing number of ministers left before the normal period of incumbency had elapsed, while others resigned from the ministry altogether.[9a] The implications of this rapid acceleration in the incidence of conflict will be considered below.

The immediate question to be answered concerns the factors and forces shaping the various incidents and occurrences of tension and conflict. There are far too many elements in the situation to be mentioned here, but in the main they derive from the nature of the Church as a voluntary organization with the consequent difficulty of the enforcement of norms: especially when the Church has failed to inculcate the norms and values which justify the authority system within which it has defined the minister's special responsibilities and powers. One expression of this difficulty is the ineffectiveness of any sanctions the minister may invoke against the recalcitrant laymen when compared with the effectiveness of the sanctions the laity can impose upon the minister. In other words, to obtain compliance with his wishes the minister must rely upon either giving or withholding ritual services and appointments[10] the value of which is not uniformly accepted by the laity. Conversely, the laymen can sanction the minister by withdrawing both their financial support and their participation in congregational activities.

Some of the ambiguities concerning the minister's role also surround the position of his wife. The laity have exacting expectations of her, assuming that she will view herself as her husband's assistant, that is 'the unpaid curate'. Her unofficial but virtually inescapable responsibilities include the holding of office in women's organizations, participation in such activities as catering and maintaining an open parsonage. A neat summary of these attitudes was expressed by one laywoman:

> If a woman is not prepared to do these things, she should not marry a minister in the first place.

In short the likelihood of a successful ministry will be increased to the extent that the minister's wife is adjusted to her pre-defined role.

Related problems arise out of the fact that the minister's job is one which lacks precise definition, is ostensibly a twenty-four-hour assignment and is carried out with maximum visibility. At the same time the minister is usually a friend, pastor, administrator, teacher, priest, social worker, and so on. Not only do these many roles impose heavy and conflicting demands upon the time, energy and wisdom of the minister; they also tax the ability of the laymen to comprehend what the minister's work is all about.

It will be clear from what has been said that such personal qualities as temperament, previous experience, general ability to get on with people are important factors in determining the minister's success in coping with latent sources of conflict. On the other hand an explanation of minister/lay conflict simply in terms of personality is too narrow a framework for dealing with the complexity of the issues involved.

Widening the Study

In unravelling the various strands contributing to these patterns it was necessary to look beyond the local congregation to social processes occurring in the total local community, and in the society as a whole. Of major importance have been the theological and organizational developments in the Methodist denomination, both

C

within Australia and internationally, especially the trend towards specialization and professionalization of the ministry.

Barool, like many small rural towns in Australia, has experienced a long period of economic and demographic stagnation. Throughout this period there has been a steady outward flow of those segments of the population from which the church drew its support, namely the small pastoralists, the orchardists and the local businessmen. It has in fact lost virtually all of its pastoralists and town-storekeepers, but still has the support of retired shop-keepers and some orchardists. As a result of these movements, what was a fairly heterogeneous congregation is now one which is much more homogeneous in membership, and smaller in numbers.[11] This group is more uniform in its evaluation, both of the minister's performance and of any innovatory proposals he may introduce.

Although there has been an increase in the number of professional and commercial itinerants resident in the town in recent years, too few of these have been Methodists to make any significant difference to the social composition of the congregation. From the minister's point of view this is perhaps unfortunate. There is some evidence to show that their presence may help to bridge the gap in social and cultural distance between the minister and the congregation, and moderate any local opposition to the minister and his policies. For example, the Clerk of Petty Sessions, one of the two professional itinerants in the congregation, provided the only consistent support for the innovations and work-orientation of one of the ministers in 1966.

The incidence of tension is also related to the declining financial buoyancy which has followed upon the emigration already noted. However, while the outward flow of prosperous Methodist families has been a principal factor in the loss of income to the church, the congregation lays much of the responsibility for this state of affairs on the shoulders of the minister. Financial decline is in fact assumed to be an accurate reflection of the failure of a minister to do his job properly. More particularly, it is taken to reflect his propensity for alienating potential supporters, or his failure to visit those who either could support the church financially or increase the support they are already providing. Indeed there seems to be a profound ambivalence in their attitudes towards the minister. They would strongly resist any suggestion that their church should be left without a ministerial appointment. On the other hand they frequently complain that it is he expenses associated with maintaining a minister which are the genesis of all their financial anxieties. As a result, undercurrents of resentment against the minister will often be found to have a basis n anxieties over finance. Indications of such feelings come to expression in not infrequent claims that the minister 'is on a good wicket', 'is in it for the money', 'is overpaid', 'doesn't know what a good day's work is'. Confusion, uncertainty and lack of understanding of the role of the minister, coupled with obscure feelings of uncertainty about the nature of the value of the church itself and its apparent lack of power as evidenced by financial decline, unite to create an atmosphere of misgiving in which the minister is the most obvious candidate for the role of 'scapegoat'.

The development of mass media of communication, of motorized transport, of increased affluence, of greater leisure and entertainment opportunities, and of widespread higher education has contributed to the lessening of the social significance of the church and of the minister's role within it.[12] It has also given rise to a developing mood of uncertainty concerning the nature and function of the church in the modern world.

In Barool, these developments are reflected in a number of changes. For example, changing and irregular habits of worship occur because many more people can now enjoy a week-end away from home or an evening watching television. People are more inclined to compare the minister's performance as a professional employee with the performance of other professional employees in the town. There is an increasing tendency for people to appraise the church pragmatically, because, having put so much money in, they expect an assessable return.

Theological Change

The relationship between ministers and laymen has been further complicated by the increasing theological distance between them. The current theological climate, which is one of widespread questioning of previously held doctrine, has drawn the minister much more into its vortex than it has the average layman. As a result ministers generally are questioning and rejecting much that is still held by the laymen as essential to their faith. A large part of the theological revolution has been concerned with the doctrine of the church, and the role of the ministry and laity. The minister, therefore, views as irrelevant to his role some of the duties laymen expect of him, while he underrates some of the activities they regard as central to their function as laymen. For example, one recent ministerial appointment in Barool placed great significance on the minister's function as trainer of laymen for what *he* regarded as their role in the community. On the other hand they rejected his understanding of their role and of his own, arguing that his time would be much better spent visiting people in the way ministers did fifty years ago.

Another growing chasm between the two parties stems from the contrast between the Barool layman's settled view of religion as 'living a decent life' and that of recent younger ministerial appointees, who are concerned to develop an articulate laity possessed of sufficient theological depth to undergird more radical political and social involvement in community and national life.

Bureaucratic and Professional Developments

Of perhaps even greater significance than local changes are developments in the Australian Methodist organization as such, and in the status of the ministry.

In Methodist understanding, the local congregation does not exist *sui generis*, but is an integral part of the connexional[13] system, deriving its legitimacy from the denomination as a whole. Because the minister is present as an authorized representative of the Connexion and because laymen will see him as such in certain situations, as for example when he seeks to uphold Conference regulations that are unpopular with the local congregation, minister/lay interaction in a local church cannot be adequately described or interpreted without reference to the wider organization. Indeed it can be argued that a proper understanding requires some familiarity with its (the Connexion's) history.

The organizational structure of Methodism has not been static; on the contrary its continuous development of specialist departments to deal with such matters as Church Extension, Christian Education and Social Work can be viewed as a mark of a burgeoning bureaucracy. Parallel with these developments has been an increase in professionalism and specialization in the ranks of the ministry. Whilst these occurrences cannot be viewed, jointly or separately, as sufficient cause for the deterioration in minister/lay relations, they are none the less important contributing factors.[14] New departments and specialized church agencies are often viewed by the rural layman as irrelevant to the local congregation to which he belongs. This disapproval is significant since these various enterprises must be financed by the local congregation. Organizational changes can in this way alienate laymen and aggravate the minister's dilemma in exercising the dual roles of organizational representative and pastor. Conference[15] decisions concerning Christian Education are a case in point. Since the turn of the century the New South Wales Conference has endeavoured to raise standards and increase efficiency in the Christian Education programmes of the local church. To achieve these goals it established a department which has steadily grown in size and importance. However, the Conference policy on Christian Education, as implemented by the Department, has met with opposition in Barool whenever its politics have departed radically from traditional Barool practices. For example, the Department's policy of Adult Education championed by a recent minister was formally rejected by the Leaders' Meeting and was the occasion of a rift between the minister and a large proportion of the congregation. Many interesting facets of this dispute have to be omitted for reasons of space. The immediately relevant consideration is that it graphically represents a case of divergent views of the respective roles of the minister and the rest of the congregation. After three years in the circuit, the minister had come to feel very strongly that the congregation could only provide effective Christian leadership in the community if it was more thoroughly informed concerning the nature of Christian faith in relation to the needs of contemporary society. He proposed to achieve this end through the inclusion of group discussion in Sunday morning worship or as an adjunct to it. His concern met with incomprehension and his initiative with opposition. Not only did the congregation object to the implication that they needed education in the faith, and to his conception of their role, but they objected strongly to any alterations in the pattern of morning worship. The minister had determined beforehand that the establishment of an Adult Christian Education programme would be a condition of his staying in the appointment, because, in his opinion, without it nothing of value could be achieved. It is not surprising therefore that the following year he sought a new appointment.

Finally, the minister's acquisition of specialist skills, high educational qualifications and other marks of membership of a professional sub-culture can widen the gap between himself and the non-professional laymen. Time and again laymen in Barool commented to the present writer: 'These university types don't understand the problems of the man on the land, and we don't understand what they are talking about. We need ministers who have knocked about a bit and know what work really means.'

On the other hand, some of Barool's younger ministers, having had a university education, and acquiring in the process similar attitudes to other professional trainees, have entered the circuit[16] situation eager to find an area of specialization. However, lay members of the church generally prefer a 'general practitioner' type of ministry along the traditional lines. As a result those ministers who attempt to take up specialized activities find that they cannot divest themselves of a number of normal circuit-minister responsibilities, and that any effort to do so meets strong lay resistance. In these circumstances the minister suffers acute frustration and the layman acute bewilderment.[17]

Conclusion

In this paper I have presented tentative findings[18] emerging from the study of the nature, frequency and origins of tension and conflict in minister/lay relations. Factors influencing such relationships are disparity in attitudes, beliefs and norms; diverse areas of origin and educational experience; the nature of political sub-structures in the congregation, the degree of congregational homogeneity, the intricacy of members' extra-church ties; and the financial viability of the denomination and the congregation. Other factors directly impinging on the minister are his diffuse role, the extent of his visibility, his wife's adjustment to or rejection of her pre-defined roles, the absence of consensus over the nature and scope of ministerial authority, and his subjection to the conflicting pressures of local congregational requirements, ecclesiastical bureaucratization, growing professionalism and specialization. In some cases a final twist is given by current theological probing which calls all of these in question.

The hypotheses which follow by no means pick up all of the problems I have enumerated. However, they point up areas in which further research, especially in other national and denominational communities, would greatly enhance the possibilities of generalization.

1. Neither the position of the minister, nor the authority necessary for the adequate fulfilment of his role is well defined. In the absence of well-established norms and sanctions, which would serve to legitimate his position and facilitate the execution of his office, he is forced to try to fill the vacuum by the force of his own personality. Conflict will increase if the minister lacks that degree of charismatic authority which must stand in for institutional authority.

2. I would further hypothesize that conflict will occur in situations in which the minister is expected to function within a number of incompatible roles, or where individuals or sub-groups of similar and considerable political significance make competing demands upon him.

3. In so far as a latent function of the minister is that of chief executive, business manager and fund raiser, congregational financial embarrassment will tend to produce the opinion that he is not doing his job properly. The condemnatory attitude that develops forms the base for the development of conflict.

4. As a professional who takes his orientation from outside the local church the minister may be politically isolated. (In Australia there is frequently only one ministerial appointee to a circuit.) By contrast, most laymen in a rural circuit have extra-church ties with a proportion of their fellow church members based on kinship, friendship, common locality and economic obligations. In a disagreement or controversy with the minister, laymen can make use of these linkages to draw on the support of other Methodists. I would hypothesize, therefore, that the greater the number and type of extra-church ties there are among members, the greater the likelihood that any disagreement or conflict between the minister and laymen will be resolved in favour of the laity.

5. If the position of the minister changes, in that his function as local representative of the denomination becomes ascendent over his function as local pastor, it can be expected that tension and conflict between the minister and the congregation will increase.

6. If either of the following two contrary lines of development takes place it can be expected that tension and conflict between

minister and laymen will occur. The first possible development is for the ministry to retain its present somewhat loose brotherhood in which divergent norms in theology and organization are tolerated. In these circumstances men with quite different approaches to their ministry can succeed one another or occupy adjacent circuits and because of their differing views will not necessarily support one another in any dispute with laymen. On the other hand the layman may be confused by differing ministerial viewpoints or appeal to one minister against another. The second possible development, stimulated by increasing professionalization and specialization, is for the ministry to become a more tightly structured and hierarchical sub-community within the total church community. It is doubtful that this second development will occur in the Methodist Church in the near future.

ACKNOWLEDGEMENTS

I am indebted to Bruce Rollins and Sister E. Woodward for making a number of excellent suggestions regarding the content and presentation of the paper. Alan Black and Dr R. L. Rooksby kindly read the draft and offered many invaluable criticisms. I am especially grateful to Professor John Nalson who at every stage of the project from which this paper has emerged has given so freely of his encouragement and expert guidance in the analysis and interpretation of data.

NOTES

Editor's note

Since this is *A Yearbook of Religion in Britain*, I may perhaps refer to my original Introduction to the 1968 issue, where I indicated a somewhat wider ambit— the Anglo-Saxon countries, America excluded. In any case, the content herein is for the most part as applicable to the British as to the Australian context.

1. By micro-study I mean the study of a limited social field at depth. Some of the advantages and limitations of this method are suggested in later sections of this paper: see pp. 60 and 61.
2. For the purposes of anonymity the congregation has been given the pseudonym the Barool Methodist Church. The pseudonym is extended to the community in which it is set, which will hereafter be referred to as Barool. The town is a service centre for the surrounding pastoral and orcharding district. In 1966 it had a population of 1,608. A further 2,500 people are serviced by the town. The Methodist Church has 95 members.
3. Analysis of data was only partially completed at the time of writing.
4. As far as conflict could be ascertained without the use of observation.
5. The above explanation of methodological emphasis should not be

interpreted as a rejection of the survey method as such. In the present study where the attempt was made to combine qualitative and quantitative approaches, a survey of subjects proved useful both to obtain information about such readily quantifiable variables as age, number and type of kinship ties, level of education and occupation, and to check on findings from observations of various aspects of the group's informal structure.

6. At no time did I try to hide the fact that I was carrying out an investigation although few, if any, understood the exact nature of the study.

7. By political significance is meant the ability of a person or a group of persons to influence the course of events in the life of the church.

8. The number of people in these categories is as follows: 6 Key Leaders, 18 Secondary Leaders, 11 Formers of Opinion, and 68 Politically Insignificant. The discrepancy between the total number here and the membership figure (see note 2) is due to the participation in Barool official meetings of members from other churches in the circuit.

9. This category includes the politically indifferent.

9a. Barool is not unique in this respect, for there is evidence of increasing frustration amongst ministers, and tension and conflict between ministers and laity, in Australian Methodism generally.

10. For example, baptism, marriage, and nomination to certain official positions.

11. Although the number of Sunday worshippers has fluctuated under different ministries, there has been an overall decline in church attendance during this century. In the first decades, it was not uncommon for 120–150 worshippers to attend an evening service. It has not been possible to get an estimate of the number attending the morning service at this time. However, by the early 'fifties the total number of people attending either morning or evening worship on any given Sunday was 70–100. By 1966 this number had fallen still further to approximately 40–50.

12. Speaking of British society Bryan Wilson has noted: 'Our society is a society in which specialization continually increases, prestige increasingly attaches to the specialist.' Although writing about teachers he comments: 'The same process has diminished the social prestige of the religious functionary.' 'The Teacher's Role: A Sociological Analysis', *British Journal of Sociology* 13.1, 1962, pp. 15–32.

13. Use of the term Connexion in the Methodist Church implies that no single congregation is an entity in itself, but derives its identity from membership in the whole denomination. This characteristic distinguishes Methodism from Congregationalism where each congregation is an independent, separate and autonomous body.

14. As J. Brothers has noted: '. . . if a social system is altered structurally, the interaction between groups within it is also affected . . .', 'Social Change and the Role of the Priest', *Social Compass* 10. 6, 1963, p. 487.

15. The Conference is an annual assembly of all ministers and equal numbers of lay representatives of circuits and other appointments from which the ministers come, for purposes of legislating the continuing life of the church under the provisions set out in General Conference legislation. The General Conference is a triennial assembly of representative ministers and laymen of the five Australian Annual Conferences and the Conferences of Fiji, Tonga and Samoa. It is the supreme legislative body of the Methodist Church of Australasia.

16. Within Methodism the main local unit is usually not a single congregation but a circuit consisting of a number of congregations under the oversight of a superintendent minister.

17. It is unfortunate that space does not permit a fuller consideration of problems inherent in the movement toward greater professionalism and specialization, for it is undoubtedly going to have a much more disruptive effect on minister/lay relations than has been the case until now. Attention needs to be given to similar changes taking place in other occupations in order to determine to what extent new developments in the ministry are part of a more widespread phenomenon.

18. I want to insist that these conclusions *are* tentative, and that, while the evidence appears to sustain them with regard to Barool, generalizations to the wider church could only be validated by much more extensive research.

4 The Faith Mission: a Study in Interdenominationalism

T. Rennie Warburton

MODERN revivalism, which one of its leading authorities[1] dates from around 1825 with the beginning of C. G. Finney's campaigns, has produced a considerable degree of co-operation across denominational lines. The itinerant preaching so typical of such men as Wesley and Whitefield was a prominent reason for its growth, especially in the USA, where the activism of a people engaged in occupying new areas and developing the country's resources, the emergence of nationalist feeling in the absence of an Established Church and the weakening of the territorial parish in a situation of high geographical mobility were elements in the changing social structure which encouraged the co-operation of Protestants from all denominations.[2] They were united by a minimal theological position – a simplified Arminianism symbolized in the line from a hymn by P. P. Bliss, who declined the hymn-singing job which Moody later gave to Sankey:

Whosoever will may come.

There were of course other features in the structure of American society which were not conducive to interdenominational evangelistic co-operation, among them the North/South rivalry and the ethnic identity of many social groups and denominations. On the whole, it was people of older American stock who were influenced by the revival movements,[3] and the growth in the last quarter of the nineteenth century of Fundamentalism, particularly the pre-millennial variety, was partly a reaction by older generations of Americans to the steady urbanization of a society which they perceived to be increasingly dominated by science, technology and hedonism.

Among the denominations themselves the extension of foreign missionary operations had the unintended consequence of bringing together personnel who, when they found themselves competing among each other in the same geographical area, soon agreed to reserve certain territories for specific organizations and later entered into active co-operation with one another.[4] A further source of interdenominationalism was the concern of many Protestant denominations with social issues, reflected in the rise first of the Anti-Slavery, and later of the Social Gospel movements. On a different level, the YMCA and the Student Christian Movement were other important developments.

Many of the social pre-conditions for denominationalism also apply to interdenominationalism. Tolerance, pluralism, the acknowledgement of the appropriate requirements of different social groups, e.g. classes, ethnic groups and communities – are all characteristic assumptions of Western democratic and industrial societies.

But interdenominationalism and, to a larger extent, the modern ecumenical movement which succeeded it, can also be understood as a response by Protestantism to a situation in which its influence was declining. The working masses of the expanding towns and cities in Britain and America were highly indifferent to organized religion and many interdenominational developments were attempts to strengthen existing denominations by evangelizing the growing urban populations. This was certainly true of the Holiness movements and of groups like the Evangelization Society and Christian Endeavour. Even movements which claimed to be *un*denominational, such as the Salvation Army and the City and Rescue Missions, were attempts by those disenchanted with the weakened spirituality of the leading denominations to galvanize the Christian community into action and to lift it to a higher spiritual plane.

The Faith Mission is a typical product of the nineteenth-century revival movement. It is primarily an evangelistic organization but is also a Holiness movement, i.e. it encourages converts to seek the Wesleyan experience of Entire Sanctification according to which they become fully saved, cleansed from sin, and receive the power of the Holy Spirit. Since its inception in 1886 it has remained interdenominational, i.e. it has no formal relation to other religious organizations and its supporters have included people from every Protestant denomination.

This paper, which is both expository and analytical, suggests that the Faith Mission is a special kind of organization which does not fit easily into existing sociological typologies.[5] Dynamic historical analysis shows that its peculiar structure continually exposes it to special kinds of strain and tension both internal and external but the movement illustrates the persistent appeal of minority religious organizations in modern industrial societies to those who are geographically and culturally isolated from the dominant urban, and primarily secular, value system. For convenience the Faith Mission is examined under four headings: (1) Organization; (2) Historical Development; (3) Structural Analysis; and (4) Social Constituency.

1. *Organization*

The Faith Mission conducts its evangelistic activities mainly in villages, country districts and small towns by means of 'pilgrims', the name given to its itinerant personnel who normally work in pairs of the same sex and hold 'missions', or series of evangelistic meetings, for periods ranging from one to five weeks. Geographically this itinerant evangelism is largely concentrated in Scotland and Ireland but also in parts of Northumberland, Durham, Yorkshire, Derbyshire, Nottinghamshire, Leicestershire and East Anglia. Other longer campaigns are held each summer in holiday resorts such as Oban, Rothesay, Portstewart and Portrush.

For administrative purposes the Mission is divided into twelve districts each supervised by a District Superintendent who is usually a male pilgrim with at least ten years' experience. Pilgrims are allotted to a district for a minimum period of three months at a time, and the location and duration of missions are decided by the Superintendent in consultation with pilgrims and normally in response to invitations from local believers. Each mission is advertised locally by means of handbills, posters and often through announcements in churches. Meetings are deliberately held at times which do not clash with those held by local churches and in recent years there has been a growing tendency to use small portable halls for this purpose, rather than church premises, community halls, schools and, in Northern Ireland, Orange Halls. During a mission pilgrims reside in the community either with a family of Faith Mission supporters or, more frequently in the past few years, in a caravan belonging to the Mission. They are expected to hold meetings most evenings of the week, to visit every home in the vicinity and to forward a weekly report to the Superintendent who draws up his own district report every quarter. Finances for the missions are provided from the movement's central fund, maintained from voluntary donations, including legacies.

From 1945 to 1965, on the average, 236 missions were held by 40 pilgrims each year. Although more missions are held in Scotland and England than in Ireland, the latter seems to be more fruitful in producing professed conversions.

Converts of missions are encouraged to join the Faith Mission Prayer Union, which is the main source of support for the Mission's operations. Its 500 or so local branches usually organize weekly meetings which are attended by members from different Protestant denominations. Total membership was estimated at around 8,000 in 1965. Each branch is led by a representative who acts as a liaison between the District Superintendent and the membership. The Superintendent is visiting speaker at about 20% of these meetings and tries to rotate among them on a quarterly basis. After an address, on an aspect of the Mission's activities, mid-monthly letters, containing information about current missions being held in the district, are read out and prayers are then offered for the movement's operations at large, as well as for specific items in the letter, e.g. for conversions in a particular village.

The Prayer Union also holds 'conferences' at various times throughout the year, though as frequently as every month in Edinburgh, Dunfermline and Belfast. They are usually conducted in the church premises of a particular Protestant denomination and are mainly attended by Prayer Union members from the district in which they are held. They consist of an afternoon or evening service, often both, and include sermons on devotional aspects of evangelical experience, testimonies and the hymns and choruses which are a typical feature of the meetings of many fundamentalist evangelical groups.

Special annual Holiness Conventions, aimed at leading believers into the experience of Entire Sanctification, are held in Edinburgh, Stornoway, Bangor (Co. Down), Larne, Ballymena and Bandon (Co. Cork). These usually last for four or five days and are led by two or three special guest preachers. They are the largest gatherings held by the Mission and in recent years the Bangor and Edinburgh ones have attracted an estimated 5,000 visitors. In most cases convention meetings are held in a large church but in Bangor five churches are often used simultaneously.

The Mission also has a youth section – the Faith Mission Young

People's Fellowship and a publishing centre whose main concern is the movement's magazine, *Life Indeed*, for merly *Bright Words*.

An important interdenominational feature of the movement is its Training Home in Edinburgh which has students from all sections of evangelical Protestantism who are taught by visiting lecturers from several Protestant denominations as well as by the small regular staff who are ex-pilgrims. Between 40 and 50 students attend each year, 75% of whom are women. Graduates of this institution are expected to become pilgrims but since 1912 only 45% have done so. Of the rest 23% went into foreign missionary work and 15% into other British religious organizations. Many of the remainder are young women who marry.

The Faith Mission is governed by a Council of over twenty members including six trustees who own the movement's property, the President of the Mission who is its leading executive officer and Editor of *Life Indeed*, four Vice-Presidents, the Principal of the Training Home and all the District Superintendents. There is also a small number of lay members, mainly businessmen. Although the entire Council gathers only once a year, most members meet at the Bangor and Edinburgh Conventions, held respectively at Easter and in late summer. But Council members are kept informed of current business through a system of sub-committees and reports. The main duties of the Council are to decide on matters of general policy, property management and appointments. Like most aspects of the Mission's affairs it is governed by a Constitution, formulated in 1930.

Theologically, the Faith Mission possesses only a minimal set of principles: a fundamentalist belief concerning the Bible, an Arminian conception of justification, a Wesleyan view of Entire Sanctification and a pre-millennial attitude to the Second Advent.

2. *Historical Development*

The Faith Mission began in Glasgow at the beginning of the last quarter of the nineteenth century. It was a period of considerable change in the structure of Scottish society. In industry, in social life, in politics and in religion, radical developments were taking place. Scotland, at least as far as its centres of industry and dense population were concerned, was rapidly losing its independence as an economic and social unity and was becoming an integral part of British industrial society.[6] Scottish economic life after 1860 had become increasingly geared to heavy industry in cities and large towns. Textiles and agriculture not only occupied a smaller proportion of the working population but their relative contribution to the country's national product declined in the face of coalmining, the iron and steel industries, engineering and shipbuilding. The 50% increase in the urban sector of the Scottish population between 1861 and 1891 has been directly attributed to large-scale migration from rural areas,[7] but Irish immigration also made an important contribution, particularly in the counties of Ayr, Dumbarton, Lanark and Renfrew,[8] which showed the greatest increases in population and which, along with Edinburgh and Fife, were the areas in which the early activities of the Mission were concentrated. Social and political reforms such as compulsory education and the extension of the franchise made great headway. The manual working classes of the new urban society became more conscious of their deprivations and developed institutionalized forms through which they could express them. The new trade unionism and the Scottish Labour Party were formed principally to further the interests of these groups. The growing popularity of professional sport, particularly association football, provided many men, both spectators and players, with a convenient aggressive outlet for the frustrations and drudgery of their new industrial life.

The Faith Mission began in 1886. Almost twenty years earlier the Second Evangelical Awakening was beginning to take effect in Scotland.[9] It received great impetus from the visits of a number of American evangelists. E. P. Hammond, Charles G. Finney and James Caughey were the earliest ones. The latter two were notable exponents of Holiness although they did not emphasize it in Scotland. Later D. L. Moody from 1873 to 1875 and again in 1882, and Torrey and Chapman at the beginning of the present century, became the principal agents of a widespread religious revival which lasted, but not without several peaks and depressions, for fifty years and involved thousands of people from almost every town and city in Britain.

The concepts of 'cultural shock' and 'relative deprivation' as employed by Holt and Glock respectively appear to have some application to this revival, particularly in Scotland.[10] The period of social change described above produced considerable disorganization in the lives of many individuals and families in their efforts to adapt themselves to the new exigencies of urban industrial life, aggravated as they were by recurrent phases of strikes and chronic unemployment. Glock's thesis that radical political movements tend to emerge among groups who perceive their economically deprived condition very clearly and thus devise rational and instrumental means of alleviating it, is pertinent to the emergence of trade unionism and a Labour Party in Scotland in the late nineteenth century. He suggested that religious movements develop when deprivations, which Glock calls 'social', 'psychic' and 'ethical', are perceived unclearly by those who suffer them but are expressed in terms of feelings of sinfulness or personal inadequacy, accompanied by a view of the social environment as a threat presented by the machinations of the powers of evil. This seems to be a useful approach to the analysis of the Scottish revival. Although evidence suggests that those who attended the revival meetings were mainly from the churchgoing sections of the community, including better-educated groups,[11] and that the masses of the cities and towns were not affected, many sections of the new urban populations were, as we have seen, recent migrants from rural areas who, as indicated by studies in North America by Holt and Mann, often provide new recruits for evangelical and Holiness religions.[12] Thus many of the participants in the Scottish revival, including regular churchgoers, seem to have been drawn to it because of the conditions of social disorganization and relative deprivation which they were experiencing in their new urban environment. In this way the religion of the churchgoers was revitalized. Another factor was the presence of large numbers of Irish immigrants in the cities. A Roman Catholic 'out-group', an unwelcome threat which produced feelings of relative deprivation, is likely to have reinforced Protestant and evangelical sentiments.

The founder of the Faith Mission, one of a myriad of small evangelistic groupings and missionary societies formed at that time, was John George Govan, the son of a successful businessman and Glasgow town councillor who was himself an evangelical preacher. Associations with William Booth of the Salvation Army and accounts he heard from people who had enjoyed the experience of Entire Sanctification at the Keswick Convention led Govan to testify to it himself. In early adulthood he had helped in his father's business and also in evangelistic meetings organized by his brother at a gospel hall in Glasgow. After accepting invitations to conduct meetings in several rural communities not far from the city and feeling that his efforts were successful, Govan agreed with a friend to commence evangelism on a permanent basis in smaller towns and villages which he felt had been neglected. When the financial donations at their first two meetings proved sufficient to meet their expenses they decided to continue according to the 'faith principle', i.e. relying on voluntary financial help. For this reason they adopted the name 'The Faith Mission' for their enterprise.

Govan saw his efforts as supplementing those of existing denominations and sought from the beginning to make his movement interdenominational. It is likely that he viewed it as the rural counterpart of the Salvation Army, which had concentrated its attention on the urban poor. Govan was soon joined by a number of assistants, including two young women, one of whom he later married. These women preachers caused some controversy among the more Calvinistic elements of the local churches but they gave a more progressive character to the movement and probably helped its appeal. It is worth noting that the Faith Mission was never conceived as a protest movement and this was an important feature of its circumstances of origin which prevented it from developing strongly sectarian tendencies.

The founder's organizing abilities were already evident when he insisted, in a rational, businesslike manner, that records and assessments of pilgrims' activities should be carefully kept and submitted to him in a weekly report. This included numbers and kinds of meetings, professions of conversion and sanctification and time spent visiting people's homes. Apart from the period 1912–22 these records have been maintained throughout the Mission's history and provide a meticulous record of its development.

Govan also sought to control the Mission's activities by issuing a booklet, *Pilgrim Life*, which included specific instructions to personnel on character development, loyalty to the Mission, methods of conducting missions and the management of finances. With other publications which have followed, such as *The Chief's* [Govan's] *Talks to Pilgrims* and *The Aim and Character of the Faith Mission Prayer Union*, they resemble the Salvation Army manuals, *Orders and Regulations* . . . and *Doctrines and Discipline*. There is little doubt that Govan modelled his movement on Salvationist lines.

But the question soon arose concerning what was to be done with new converts at the end of a campaign and Govan's response to it determined the Faith Mission's later development in a far-reaching way. He decided that converts

> ... needed more looking after than ... anticipated, and that very few of the churches they were connected with gave them either the sympathy, spiritual teaching, or Christian work that was necessary to healthy Christian life.[13]

He was against setting up another denomination but, without discouraging converts from attending the services of existing denominations, he formed the Faith Mission Prayer Union in July 1887.

By 1888 local representatives had been appointed in Prayer Union branches and among their tasks was the enlisting of members on an annual basis. During its second year the Mission attracted a considerable number of followers in the mining communities of Fifeshire and Govan appointed a District Pilgrim to look after the Prayer Union branches in that area. Careful attempts were made to hold meetings at times other than those of the denominations and the Mission was in this way able to keep controversy with them to a minimum.

Although, according to McLoughlin, many of them had made concessions to Arminianism during the previous fifty years, Holiness doctrine was still both new and unacceptable to most Scottish Presbyterians who were typically Calvinistic in outlook. This accounts for much of the opposition and lack of support which Govan's early activities received from the denominations and his emphasis on the Holiness experience continued to lead to some tension. Pamphlets were written attacking the Mission's position on this score and some groups opposed the emotionalism which they felt was reflected in the movement's use of enthusiastic songs, musical instruments and a lack of dignity in the conduct of services.

Despite this criticism the Mission continued to flourish and by 1890 there were twenty-eight pilgrims. Conventions and conferences were begun and the magazine *Bright Words* was taken over from its former independent publishers in London. By 1891 there were five districts in Scotland, including ninety-five branches with a total of around 3,000 members. The rapidity of this early growth rate was not continued for at least thirty years.

In the 1890's the Mission began evangelism in Ireland and met with immediate success in terms of numbers of professions of conversion and a remarkable increase in financial donations. Also at this time Govan wished to establish a training home, mainly because he was dissatisfied with the training and performance of his pilgrims. This was hardly surprising, for many of them had received little formal education. He held short-term courses each lasting several weeks but it was not possible to establish a training home until 1912. One reason for the delay was shortage of funds. The movement's following at that time seems to have been readier to support foreign missionary activity by other movements and only by reducing emphasis on that area did Govan cause contributions to be made for the training establishment.

A more bureaucratic approach towards the organization of the movement's affairs was adopted in the 1890's when District Pilgrims were given oversight of missions as well as Prayer Union branches. Govan was assisted at this time by his brother and they were both divested of some responsibilities by these changes. Certain financial arrangements were handed over to District Pilgrims, enabling Govan himself to concentrate on general oversight and training and his brother on editing and publishing the magazine and other literature.

But in the years immediately preceding 1900 these organizational changes underwent further revision. In response to a decline in attendances at meetings and fewer conversions and donations, Govan took some of the financial and business responsibilities away from the District Pilgrims, enabling them to concentrate more on the pastoral and evangelistic side.

There were controversies which hindered the Mission's development at this time. Pilgrims were dismissed for adopting alien theological views and in one case for moral turpitude. Schism occurred in 1901 when three or four pilgrims, under the influence of Cooney and Irvine, decided while conducting missions in Ireland to embark on independent evangelism. There is evidence to suggest that they were not in sympathy with Holiness teachings and that they felt that the Faith Mission, contrary to its faith principles, was becoming over-organized. Irvine was also directly opposed to fraternizing with denominations which had espoused what he saw as a lukewarm, liberal Christianity. The breakaway group has since come to be known as the Cooneyites and has acquired a considerable following in North America.[14]

These developments resulted in the Faith Mission being subjected to hostile criticism by Scottish and Irish newspapers. It was also alleged to be compromising its interdenominational position by holding baptismal services, but Govan strongly denied the charges.

The Mission's leaders did, however, offer some explanations as to why it was not making much headway. One was that there was a widespread migration to cities and towns by potential converts. It was also pointed out that Prayer Union branches were suffering from lapsed commitment and an attempt was made to activate them by issuing detailed instructions on how to prepare for and help a local mission by prayer, advertising and participation. However, the more favourable response to the Mission's activities in Ireland compared to England and Scotland was noted by the movement's leaders at this time and it has been a continuing feature of the Mission's growth.

Further organizational modifications took place in 1912, when Govan returned to the movement after a period of illness and decided to spread responsibility for decision-making among senior personnel. He formed a Council for the first time and included all the District Superintendents, as they were newly named, as well as a small number of lay members. This step, together with the establishment of the training home in the same year, represented the most significant transition which the movement has undergone from its former more loosely and autocratically organized system of operations to a more routinized oligarchical form, in line with the organization of older and larger religious bodies.

The inspirational vision of Govan was given more institutionalized expression through the Council. The ownership of valuable property necessitated by the purchase of training premises and the demand to ensure that the Mission would continue after its founder's death required the adoption of methods consistent with the legal framework of secular society. A Deed of Trust was drawn up to ensure that the property would continue to be owned by the Mission's representatives and there was much discussion about a constitution to establish the movement on a legal basis.

Although some of these developments are similar to the familiar process which results in some sect-like bodies becoming more like denominations, they were actually attempts to avoid such pressures and to ensure the Mission's persistence as an interdenominational evangelistic organization.

The movement extended its operations to East Anglia in 1913 and, although the first World War was seen to constitute something of a threat to its future – schools and halls were used for housing military personnel, money was scarce, male pilgrims were likely to be in short supply – the war years brought success to the Mission's operations and only publishing had to be suspended. Its stand on pacifism was one which allowed individual personnel to reach their own decisions about enlistment. In Northern Ireland, where the Elim Pentecostal Movement was developing at this time, the Mission participated in a widespread evangelical revival, but in Scotland and in the new district in England it continued to receive a moderate response.

The early 1920's, however, were a peak period in the Mission's history, conversions during 1923 reaching to almost 4,000. The prevailing economically depressed conditions appear to provide a partial explanation.

Govan died in 1927 and was succeeded by his brother, Horace, who had been editor of *Bright Words*. The Mission became increasingly concerned with its own survival and, after a small donation had been received towards providing a stipend for retired personnel, a Retired Workers' Fund was opened. But the increasing financial prosperity which characterized the Mission at this time was not merely because more people were converted but may have resulted from the gifts of businessmen who were on the Council.

In 1930 the discussions about a constitution materialized and the Mission also produced a statement on the origin and control of the movement. The constitution made provision for the appointment of successive presidents by the Council, as well as the running of the Mission in the president's absence.[15] The Council was also given statutory power over the acceptance of students into training and the appointment of pilgrims. Partly to offset the trend towards bureaucratic centralization provision was made for changes in the constitution only after the approval of at least 75% of pilgrims with five years' standing.

Some threat to the Mission's interdenominational position was presented during this period when a lay member of the Council bequeathed a gospel hall in Dunfermline to the Mission. It was an unforeseen consequence of deepening commitment of the movement's followers. In spite of some criticism, directed at the Mission on the grounds that in maintaining the hall it was compromising its position, the building has been retained and is used for regular services and as a district headquarters, although meetings are held so as not to clash with the times of services held by other denominations.

The Mission was again heavily criticized by some denominations for its enthusiastic approach. 'Emotional feelings, carrying a big, fat

Bible under your arm, hanging texts of Scripture in your bedrooms and holding certain dogmatic beliefs' were all denounced. The Mission's leaders responded by emphasizing the extent to which it had set out to differ from existing denominations and declaring that 'humble supplication before God' was infinitely preferable to 'ecclesiastical arrangement'.[16] But it seems that the Mission had not yet become fully respectable.

Allegations that missions were being held in towns against the movement's principles were met with statements that its evangelists had always felt free to respond to invitations in exceptional circumstances and that the results amply justified this. In fact urban missions have never comprised more than 10% of missions held in any one year.

The Mission appears not to have been greatly affected by the revival activity of the 1930's, although operations in Northern Ireland continued to produce a more than satisfactory response. In 1936 the Fiftieth Jubilee Anniversary of the Mission was celebrated and the letters of appreciation from Queen Mary and from the Moderators of the Irish and Scottish Presbyterian Churches were received with pride. A special book of essays was published comprising a review of the movement's history and several reminiscences of revival times by older personnel. A second magazine called *Life Indeed*, containing purely evangelistic articles, was issued from 1930 to 1939. Considerable sums were put in the Retired Workers' Fund. Taken together, these developments are further evidence of institutionalization and of the movement's increasing preoccupation with its internal affairs and future security.

On the death of Horace Govan in 1932 the presidency had been given to J. A. A. Wallace, a landowner and retired businessman, and it appears, in view of the fact that two experienced pilgrims with forty years' experience were not given this position, that the Mission may have been intent on improving its position among the respectable denominations and churches by ensuring that the social status and acceptability of its leader were on a par with the denominational ministers. By 1938 the President was able to report that

. . . concerning the Mission's work in general there is an increasing confidence among the ministers of nearly all denominations. Many who at one time stood aloof are showing signs of sympathy and not infrequently give help in the work.[17]

In the following year the movement's respectability was enhanced when D. W. Lambert, M.A., who had held the post of tutor at the Methodist Cliff College, was made principal of the Training Home. In 1944 the training course was extended from one to two years and the curriculum expanded to include Church History, the Theology of an Evangelist, Homiletics, Child Evangelism, Literature, Nursing and Homecraft. The institution was renamed the 'Faith Mission Training Home and Bible College'.

World War II seems not to have affected the Mission in any serious way. Its official legal status enabled it to withstand some of the potential threats of war, notably in terms of the exemption from military service which was available to male pilgrims as full-time religious officers. There were 'blackout' restrictions and the ban on large assemblies prevented conventions from being held, but otherwise the Mission's activities continued and local conferences increased in number and were unusually well attended.

After the war J. G. Eberstein, a Cambridge graduate, who was certainly the most highly educated, if not the most experienced, pilgrim, became College Principal and President. He later relinquished the training duties but has remained President since 1947 and Editor of the magazine since 1934.

By far the most important event in the movement's post-war history was the Lewis revival of 1949–51. Its beginnings were somewhat independent of the Mission's activities but a senior pilgrim, Rev. Duncan Campbell, was deeply involved almost from the outset. It appears to have begun during a prayer meeting in the Church of Scotland parish church in Barvas, Lewis, in the later months of 1949. Deep concern had been expressed by local ministers at the poor spiritual condition of the community, especially among the youth. The revival was confined to the rural parts of Lewis, Harris and Bernera. Stornoway, the largest community in this area, appears to have been untouched. There were some typically noteworthy events in this revival such as weeping, trance phenomena and other 'physical manifestations'; for instance, it was claimed that houses shook during prayer meetings and that people rolled on the ground in agonized conviction of sin. Campbell and his helpers held a large number of services, many of them lasting until the early morning hours, and the Mission's record of professions of conversion increased considerably at this time.

There are some obvious factors to be considered when attempting to explain this phenomenon. One is the steady urbanward migration of younger people to Stornoway and to the Scottish mainland which had been occurring throughout the present century and which not only reduced the overall number of the rural inhabitants of Lewis but resulted in a highly aging population. Unemployment was high, around 25%, in the years after World War II, mainly due to a decline in the tweed and herring fishing industries, as well as in agriculture.[18] But the familiar relationship between economic depression and religious revival provides only a partial understanding. Culturally Lewis may be said to be on the fringe of British society. Local social life includes none of the typically urban forms of entertainment and the level of cultural sophistication is relatively low. Life is narrowly centred around crofting, family and church and the people lead a harsh but seriously Puritanical sort of existence with only a minimum of frivolity. Strong Protestant-Catholic rivalry between neighbouring islands is also found in this area.

Any adequate explanation must take into account the multiple effects of all these elements in the situation, as well as a strong tradition of superstition and something of a history of revival phenomena.[19] One curious fact is that, although the Mission was closely involved in the development of the revival, it produced little expansion in the number of Prayer Union branches, even though several of the converts became pilgrims. A major reason for this was the opposition encountered from the Free Church of Scotland, a deeply Calvinist organization which saw the revival as a disguised attempt by the Church of Scotland to extend its influence in the area and therefore discouraged its members from joining local prayer groups.

In 1957 the President, commenting on the movement's progress, observed that

> many a work truly begun in the Spirit has developed on stereotyped lines, with the resultant loss of vision, lack of vitality and leakage of power.

He hoped this would not happen to the Faith Mission. Two years later he wrote:

> As an organization of necessity increases with the growth and development of the work, it is possible for the spontaneity and freedom of younger days to lessen. May this never be so of our beloved Mission . . .

Continuing to show his awareness of the dangers of the routinization process, he referred in 1964 to the third generation of a movement, when its workers are people who did not know the founder, as the stage when 'many a movement has settled down and begun to live on the traditions of the past'.

These observations appear to be tardy. Already in 1947 a Former Pilgrims' Fellowship had been formed to enable contact and correspondence to be maintained among retired and present pilgrims. In 1955 a film was made to introduce people to those without first-hand knowledge of it. The Young People's Fellowship which originated at a house party in 1960 is further evidence of the movement's attempt to move with the times and to solve some of its recruitment problems by providing specially attractive activities for young people. Since 1948 the Mission has paid full National Insurance contributions for its personnel and, judging by the interest accruing from investments in the Retired Workers' Fund, the economic security provided for personnel is considerable. Here is evidence of the Mission's concern with its past and of its having settled down. The Retired Workers' Fund, including its investments, suggests some compromise of the Mission's 'faith principle'.

But the Mission has done well financially in recent years. All the district pilgrims are provided with a house and car and several portable halls and caravans have been bought for use during missions. But numbers of professed conversions have fallen and, although a new district was formed in Yorkshire and the Midlands in 1964, the movement claims success more and more in terms of its contribution of personnel to world-wide evangelization. It has been fortunate in continuing to attract large proportions of students to the College from Northern Ireland.

Many of these developments suggest that the Mission's leaders, perhaps unintentionally, have become as concerned with its status image and preservation as with its original evangelistic goals. The provision of economic security in the form of the Retired Workers' Fund makes for feelings of comfort, cosiness and respectability which have rarely been associated with successful, enthusiastic and continuing revivalism. While the Faith Mission has successfully preserved its interdenominational character it has not been without unintended consequences. The cultivation of a more respectable image has required it to adapt to the legal requirements of the wider society and to the security needs of its personnel. This has resulted in the loss of much of that pristine fervour and spontaneity which the processes of routinization and formalization always tend to erode.

3. *Structural Analysis*

The Faith Mission appears to possess many of the features characteristic of the typical conversionist sect which has been shown to be
most susceptible to development into denominational form, partly
as a consequence of its Arminian theology.[20] Although several of
the points made in the preceding historical section – e.g. an increasing concern for the spiritual condition of the young, the establishment of a training institution, the legalization of the movement's
official status and the routinization of procedure – suggest that
there has been some evolution of this kind, there is much to indicate
that the Mission has always possessed traits which could place it
outside the sect-denominational typology.

Most attempts to delineate the typical sect include some reference
to separatism, in such areas as worship, organization or social
practices. The Mission is separatist only in one or two very special
senses, e.g. it is independent of all other organized bodies and con-
ceives its role in very narrow terms as primarily the evangelization
of rural communities. To the extent that it encourages its followers
partially to withdraw from the worldliness of the wider secular
society it is separate only in the manner of most fundamentalist and
Holiness groups. It is clearly not sectarian in the sense that it claims
possession of a truth which is denied to all other groups or that there
can be no salvation outside of it. Its exclusiveness is only part of the
wider exclusiveness of movements of the evangelically converted.

Although it does subscribe to an ideal of perfection the Faith
Mission has always refrained from laying down more than minimal
norms of conduct and principles of doctrine, as a means of preserving its interdenominational commitment. Indeed, it has been
pointed out by one of the Mission's District Superintendents that
the more emotional and enthusiastic behaviour of some of the movement's Northern Irish followers might be unacceptable to many of
the more sober and undemonstrative Anglicans in the English districts. Since the two sections are not likely to have much contact,
this situation presents no danger to the future of the Mission.
Similar variations have been found in other movements.[21]

Moreover, while it is essentially a lay kind of organization, the
movement has laid no claims to being democratic – the 75% majority
vote of experienced pilgrims required to change the constitution
being merely a token – and has always been run along the lines of a

centralized bureaucracy, albeit with delegated authority. But although the Mission's pilgrims have role-commitments similar to those of the ministry, and have considerable contact with members of that profession, they see themselves as evangelists rather than clergy and in so far as they do not preside over such rites as baptism, marriage and Holy Communion, their role does not correspond in certain important respects with that of the minister.

In its relations with secular society the movement is only hostile to the extent that Puritanical proscriptions typical of evangelical fundamentalism are applied to such things as professional sport, the cinema, tobacco and alcohol consumption and the use of certain cosmetics and beauty aids.

Although the commitment demanded of Faith Mission believers is total rather than partial, they are not expected to renounce their secular employment or their unconverted next of kin but their faith is supposed to relate to and pervade the whole range of their social interactions and relationships. They attend more religious meetings than the general churchgoing population and they are expected to witness to their faith during their routine daily social contacts. These are qualities which have been associated with sectarianism but in this respect the Mission differs little from members of the wider evangelical community.

If one takes membership of the Prayer Union as a criterion for membership of the movement, it is based on a conception of personal status, i.e. profession of conversion, and is renewed on an annual basis to remind the member of his commitments and obligations to the Mission's activities. But there seem to have been no cases of expulsion and the operation of official disciplinary measures of social control has never been prevalent. This sectarian characteristic is therefore not fully developed.

In its early days, like most of the newly founded nineteenth-century groups, it claimed not to be another sect or denomination, and in a very peculiar way which is untypical of most other groups it appears to have succeeded in maintaining some important features of its pristine position.[22] Whereas most regular churchgoers give allegiance to one denomination at a time, most of those who support the Faith Mission are members of two organizations, i.e. their denomination and the Faith Mission itself. This is true in spite of the exceptional circumstances where the Mission holds regular Sunday meetings on its own premises, and it actively encourages believers to attend some denominational services as well as its own. To many of its followers it offers a communal type of religion to complement the more associational nature of the denominations.[23] It is in this very special respect that the Mission clearly lies outside the sect-denomination typology, although like the Quaker movement it maintains co-existent sectarian and denominational traits.

The Faith Mission's special status has not been preserved without difficulties and the movement has never been free from certain pressures and tensions in its relationship with the secular society and with other religious bodies. The interdenominational path is not easy to tread and many of the Mission's opponents have sought to increase the difficulties. We have already referred to the gospel halls and church premises which were bequeathed to the Mission by faithful adherents. In the sphere of pilgrims' missionary activity one of the sources of tension has been the holding of meetings on the premises of a local evangelical church, since it has tended to produce allegations that the Faith Mission is indeed attached to an official denomination. Increasing financial donations in the post-war affluent society have enabled the Mission to meet this problem in certain areas, including Northern Ireland, by purchasing its own mobile gospel halls, the largest of which can accommodate over fifty people at a meeting. Caravans are also being used to avoid pilgrims having to reside with a local minister or other supporter.

The teaching of Holiness also presents special problems, including the dilemma of whether to invest resources and talents in the salvation of the unconverted or the sanctification of believers. While the Mission has always stood for Holiness, it has never seen itself primarily as a Holiness movement and has in the main confined this aspect of its teaching to the annual convention meetings. Rational organization such as this has been important as a means of preserving the Mission's identity.

Relations with other Holiness bodies have also been limited. In 1942 when British Holiness movements met to form a National Holiness Association the Faith Mission, although it was represented in early discussions, chose not to attach itself to the national organization. There is other evidence which suggests that the Mission, or at least its official leadership, has been concerned to maintain some social distance and to preserve a sense of respectability in its relations with other Holiness groups. Govan's spiritual experience was greatly influenced by the Keswick Convention and he and his successors have always maintained close relations with the League of Prayer. The Keswick Convention takes a moderate view of Holiness experience and in recent years has come to see it as a process and the result of increasing self-control, rather than as an instantaneous and final experience which is the typical teaching of most Holiness groups.[24] These differences appear to correlate with the different social composition of Holiness movements. Supporters of the Keswick Convention and the League of Prayer are predominantly from Southern England and appear to be of higher social status than those of the Church of the Nazarene, which is the only national Holiness movement in Britain and has a predominantly lower-class following. Relations between the Church of the Nazarene and the Faith Mission have never been very close and, except for the Keswick Convention and the League of Prayer, there have been few references in Faith Mission publications to Holiness movements and their activities.

An interdenominational, as distinct from undenominational, pose necessitates a concern for status and respectability since it demands that the movement be acceptable to most denominational groups. Govan was aware of this from the outset and sought to guard against all forms of extremism in the Mission's preaching, conduct of services and social teachings. He therefore laid down only a minimal set of doctrinal principles. Govan, as one might expect, given his middle-class origins, was never a fiery, demonstrative preacher, and only in certain sections of the Mission, such as Northern Ireland, do services normally reach a high level of enthusiasm and emotional excitement. Most meetings are conducted in an informal but restrained atmosphere which involves more active congregational participation, especially in vociferous singing, than the quietly formal services found among the larger denominations. There is evidence that the Mission's personnel are instructed not to encourage extreme emotionalism in meetings, especially those dealing with Holiness.

In the publications field, also, the Mission adopts a restrained approach. The format of its magazine is sober and respectable and few of its articles include the inflammatory evangelical language found among the publications of many Holiness and revivalistic groups.

But it is in the area of leadership that the respectable self-image of the movement has been particularly stressed. John George Govan, his brother Horace, Wallace who was the Mission's third president, and Eberstein, his successor, have all been men of high social status and their personal qualities have made them thoroughly acceptable to members of the ministerial profession. They have never put the Mission in danger of being led by fanatical extremists.

Also relevant in this regard are the men who are invited to give weekly lectures in the College. Almost all of them are denominational ministers in Edinburgh and in recent years around 50% of them have been university graduates. They are listed in all issues of the movement's official magazine and undoubtedly enhance its status among Protestant denominations, as well as providing an educated, professional model with which students can identify.

It is clear from the above that the Mission is neither denomination nor sect. Although co-operation with and tolerance towards denominations has been seen as a typical feature of denominationalism,[25] the fact that most Mission followers are members of denominations and that the movement does not replace, but rather supplements, believers' denominational activities, makes its position atypical. While it does not possess certain prominent sectarian characteristics it performs some functions in contemporary society which have been attributed to sectarian movements. These will be illustrated in the final section.

4. *Social Constituency*

The social composition and appeal of the Faith Mission may be looked at in the light of data on conversionist movements which have shown that they flourish in times and among regions of economic depression. While there is a certain amount of evidence to suggest that the Faith Mission increased its following in its early years during periods of economic distress, particularly unemployment, there is little to indicate that the movement has recruited large numbers from among the economically disinherited since 1923 when the number of recorded professions of conversion reached a peak of almost 4,000 adults. Annual recorded conversions fell from the above figure to around 2,300 in 1927, to 1,500 in 1931, to less than 1,000 during World War II, since when they have varied from 500–800 per year.

In this regard, however, the Mission's continual success in Northern Ireland is remarkable. Except for the 1949–51 Lewis revival and in spite of the fact that fewer missionary campaigns have been held in Ireland, it has consistently produced during the past thirty years from 50 to 90% more recorded professions of conversion than England and Scotland. At least 80% of all Irish professions occur in Ulster and the crowds of 5,000 which regularly attend the annual Bangor convention meetings and the far greater and steadily increasing number of Prayer Union members in that region suggest that many converted believers in Northern Ireland continue their interest in the Mission. Since 1933 at least 50% of students in the Training College have come from Ulster.

While any attempt to explain this phenomenon must include much speculation in the absence of more data and rigorous historical analysis, it is clear that the Faith Mission's appeal in Northern Ireland is only part of the wider popularity there of evangelical fundamentalist religion since the awakening of 1859.[26] Among the more obvious elements in the social structure of that region which have probably helped evangelicalism is the intense Protestant/ Catholic rivalry which has brought together Protestants of all denominations. Irish Presbyterianism has also, unlike its Scottish counterpart, never been perceived as being linked to the British establishment and, apart from Roman Catholicism, there has been no outgroup to which Ulster Presbyterianism has been opposed. Its development was greatly influenced by the migrating Covenanters from the Scottish lowlands. Moreover, evangelicalism is a part of the strong folk culture in rural Ulster, and that area has some similarity to Lewis in that both are considerably removed from the mainstream of British social life.

The anti-worldliness of fundamentalism has very often been a protest against the encroachment of urban values on rural culture, hence the unacceptability of the dance-hall, the cinema and other synthetic symbols of urban culture, such as cosmetics. This kind of protest is a means of preserving a folk culture in areas where religious values and activities conducted under religious auspices occupy a large proportion of leisure time. In such areas religious institutions have many social functions and are frequently the only means of providing recreation and entertainment.

Wilson, in discussing the Elim movement in Northern Ireland, has observed that the intellectual climate of small towns and rural areas makes for a favourable response to revivalism. He claims that the underdeveloped state of sophisticated public opinion, the absence of a developed critical sense, acceptance of authority and a background tradition of faith in the Bible produce conditions in which fundamentalism can flourish.[27] These conditions are often reinforced, he maintains, when people become aware that such traditional standards have declined elsewhere.

While these remarks are pertinent to the Faith Mission's situation in Northern Ireland, they only outline some of the necessary conditions for the Mission's appeal, since many similar observations can be made about other rural areas of Britain, e.g. the Scottish Highlands and East Anglia, where the Mission appears to be conspicuously less successful.

Any adequate analysis of Northern Irish fundamentalism must also include a historical account of the acceptance of an Arminian type of theology by Scotch-Irish Presbyterianism. In the year preceding the 1857 revival the Presbyterian Church in Ireland sent two distinguished representatives to observe the awakening in America and their accounts were the first of many which, according to Orr, 'tended greatly to quicken the minds of both ministers and people' in Ulster, thus paving the way for the outbreak of revival there.[28] It is worth noting that American Presbyterianism had by this time thoroughly accepted the itinerant evangelism of the revivalists, mainly through the impact of George Whitefield.[29] But Baptist and Methodist evangelists had much success among the Scotch-Irish Presbyterians in America in the eighteenth century and Methodism, even in Wesley's time, had flourished in Northern Ireland. These observations, therefore, suggest that the present-day continuing popularity of evangelical religion in Ulster cannot be adequately explained without a historical analysis going back at least to the middle of the eighteenth century and perhaps to the mass migrations from the Scottish lowlands to Ulster a hundred years previously.

The re-evangelization of areas which evidenced revivals in previous times has also produced many Faith Mission followers. Northern Ireland includes many places which were evangelized by Jeffreys in the 1925–35 period when the Elim Pentecostal movement flourished. Apart from the 1857 awakening, the visits of Moody in 1873 and Torrey in 1904 to Belfast were earlier times of revival. East Anglia and Lewis are other areas where Faith Mission enterprise fifteen or twenty years after a previous revival period has brought success, although it is not known to what extent the same groups, or those in contact with them, were involved in each period. But, assuming

D

that many of those who have recently been brought into the Faith Mission were converted during adolescence in the 1930's, the age structure of the Prayer Union should provide some indication. A 20% sample survey, using District Superintendents as informants, divided members into those over and those under 35 years of age. For the Mission as a whole the percentage over 35 was 63 but among the regional variations were those of 58% for Northern Ireland, 73% for England and Scotland and 82% for East Anglia. Only the latter case might be evidence of re-evangelization; there was a revival outbreak there in the 1930's. But these figures are not easily interpreted and a division into those over and under 50 or 55 might have been more illuminating. Unfortunately, such detailed information was not available.

A number of studies have documented the attractions of conversionist groups for women, and this seems to apply to the Faith Mission. In the sample study of Prayer Union members women were found to outnumber men in every district. In the English and Scottish sections together the percentage of women was 68, which is similar to that found in the Emmanuel Holiness movement in 1961 as well as that estimated for the Elim Pentecostal movement in the 1950's.[30] But in Ireland, and in the Highlands of Scotland, though women are still in the majority, the preponderance is considerably smaller. In these latter areas religion generally retains a higher level of popularity and has not suffered the general decline which has occurred in certain kinds of religiosity in British life during the present century. This seems to provide one kind of explanation for the continuing appeal of the Mission to males in these areas.

While no systematically gathered evidence is available on the occupational status of Faith Mission supporters and their families, observation at meetings of all types and conversations with senior members of the organization who have been familiar with the rank and file for many years indicate that they are recruited from manual working groups. Although there are examples of professionals belonging to the Prayer Union and every social status group is represented the vast majority are, as one informant put it, 'ordinary folk'. But they are not from the poorest sections of the community and appear to be of higher socio-economic standing than followers of Pentecostal groups, although the Mission is to some extent prevented from recruiting many white collar workers and their families since they do not predominate in rural areas.

Substantial evidence on socio-economic composition was, however, available regarding students in the Faith Mission Training Home and Bible College. A remarkably high proportion of their fathers were either skilled manual workers or farmers, the latter being mainly small-holders, predominantly in Ulster. In the period 1934–60 only five of 345 students came from higher professional homes, including those of two accountants. Only 32 were from lower professions, managerial or self-employed business groups.

About one-third of the 98 male students who entered between 1934 and 1960 were upwardly mobile, assuming that missionaries, pilgrims, evangelists and Nonconformist ministers are classified in the Registrar-General's Class 2. Many of these were from Ireland.

Forty-three of the 98 male students since 1934 had received only an elementary school education and a further 27 said they had received 'secondary' education which probably means 'Secondary Modern'. Only one of these had received higher education. This suggests, with the evidence in the previous paragraph, that entry into the training institution and into the personnel of the Faith Mission provides numbers of young men with opportunities for social mobility which would otherwise be denied them in the wider secular society. The occupations of the male students before entry into the College have been predominantly farming and skilled manual. There were no professionals and very few unskilled manual workers.

Among women students the situation is different since about half of them were either nurses (some in training) or teachers. Many of the women were therefore upwardly mobile before going to the College, although religious activities may provide compensation for feelings of failure in their job or in their affectual relationships. Consistently around two-thirds of women pilgrims leave during the first five years, many of them to marry ministers, pilgrims or Prayer Union members.

Denominational representation in the Faith Mission includes most of the Protestant groups. Detailed information was available only on one district of the Prayer Union (Yorkshire and the Midlands) where Methodists predominated, followed by Anglicans, Baptists and other Free Churches, with English Presbyterians, Brethren and Pentecostalists making minor contributions. In East Anglia, according to the District Superintendent, Baptists, Anglicans and Congregationalists form the majority and Methodists are few. In Southern Ireland another knowledgeable informant said that 75%

were Methodists with Presbyterians, Baptists and Brethren accounting for the remainder. In Scotland generally, the Church of Scotland and other Presbyterian bodies (except the Free Church of Scotland), Methodists, Baptists, Congregationalists and Brethren comprise over 90% of the membership. In Northern Ireland the Presbyterians dominate, closely followed by Baptists, Methodists, Pentecostalists and Church of Ireland representations.

From 1912 to 1960 'Presbyterians' (23%), Baptists (14%), Methodists (12%), Independent groups including many gospel halls (11%), the Church of England (8%) and the Church of Ireland (8%) account for over 75% of all students. The remainder were from the United Free Church of Scotland, the Church of Scotland, the Holiness bodies, the Congregationalists and the Brethren.

The Faith Mission is therefore a genuinely interdenominational movement which operates on the fringe of Protestant church life and for most of its followers it supplements their activity in many orthodox denominations. For a number of other supporters, e.g. in Dunfermline, Fort William, Ballymena and several other places in Northern Ireland where the mission owns gospel halls, it replaces the denomination as the focal point of religious activity. Unfortunately no evidence is available concerning the relative degree of commitment on the part of supporters to their denomination as compared to the Faith Mission and there is therefore no way of knowing how successful the Mission is in encouraging them to attend denominational services in addition to its own.

But local denominations have actively supported the Mission's evangelistic operations in recent years by announcing its meetings in their services, encouraging people to attend and even offering organized help in such forms as door-to-door visitation. As has been shown, however, the same denomination may be highly co-operative in one area, but hostile in another; for instance, the Methodists are among the movement's keenest supporters in Eire but in East Anglia have little time for it.

The Faith Mission persists for some reasons which are applicable to other religious minorities. The homely and spontaneous atmosphere of its services, and the absence of formality make it very congenial to its lower-class following. In filling some of the gaps in the social structure of British society it offers compensation for emotional, cultural and socio-economic deprivation to those people for whom evangelical fundamentalism is culturally appropriate. In demanding relatively total commitment from its followers it replaces or supports elements of their value-system with a distinctive *Weltanschauung*.

But in performing these functions it has also maintained a certain respectability which is part of its appeal, particularly to upper working and lower middle class groups. The refusal of its leaders to modify its clear-cut goals has enabled it to remain interdenominational, and to resist some of the more typical pressures towards sectarianism. Its fairly loose theology makes it acceptable to a wide circle within Protestantism but, most important, its highly rational organization, in which such things as the dissemination of Holiness teaching and the support of foreign missions[31] have been deliberately underdeveloped or confined to certain specific occasions, has enabled it to pursue its major goal, rural evangelism, without being obliged to compromise its cherished interdenominational principle. Its outreach is diminishing in terms of the numbers it affects, but by mobilizing and satisfying those who remain and continue to come in it is likely to persist for some time. Its organizational distinctiveness will prevent it from amalgamating with other groups and so long as it can continue to recruit personnel its future seems to be a secure one.

NOTES

1. W. B. McLoughlin, Jr., *Modern Revivalism*, New York: Ronald Press, 1959.

2. K. S. Latourette, *Christianity in a Revolutionary Age*, Vol. III, The Nineteenth Century Outside Europe, London: Eyre and Spottiswoode, 1961, pp. 96–100.

3. *Ibid.*, p. 138.

4. Bryan R. Wilson, *Religion in Secular Society*, London: Watts, 1966, pp. 144–9.

5. The paper is a modification of a section of the author's doctoral thesis, T. R. Warburton, *A Comparative Study of Minority Religious Groups, with special reference to Holiness and related movements in Britain in the last 50 years*, Ph.D., London, 1966.

6. George S. Pryde, *Scotland from 1603 to the Present Day*, Edinburgh: Nelson, 1962, pp. 245ff.

R. L. Mackie, *A Short History of Scotland*, Edinburgh: Oliver and Boyd, 1962, pp. 267ff.

7. *Depopulation in Rural Scotland*, Regional Research Unit, Department of Health for Scotland, 1951.

8. Pryde, *op. cit.*, p. 251.

9. J. Edwin Orr, *The Second Evangelical Awakening in Britain*, London and Edinburgh: Marshall, Morgan and Scott, 1955.

10. J. B. Holt, 'Holiness Religion, Cultural Shock and Social Reorganization' _American Sociological Review_ 5.4, 1940, pp. 740–47.

Charles Y. Glock, 'The Role of Deprivation in the Origin and Evolution of Religious Groups', in R. Lee and M. Marty (eds.), _Religion and Social Conflict_ New York and London: Oxford University Press, 1964, pp. 24–36.

11. McLoughlin, _op. cit._, pp. 200–203.

12. Holt, _art. cit._; W. E. Mann, _Sect, Cult and Church in Alberta_, University of Toronto Press, 1955.

13. From Govan's account of the movement's beginnings in _Bright Words_ Edinburgh, July 1893, p. 179.

14. An account of the Cooneyites in North America whose author was unaware of the movement's origins is to be found in: K. Crow, _The Invisible Church_, M.A. Thesis, University of Oregon, 1963.

15. It is interesting to note that similar matters of concern were being resolved in the Salvation Army at this time. R. Robertson, 'The Salvation Army: the Persistence of Sectarianism', 2 in B. R. Wilson (ed.), _Patterns of Sectarianism_ London: Heinemann, 1967, pp. 76–82.

16. Faith Mission Annual Report, _Bright Words_, Edinburgh, November 1929.

17. Faith Mission Annual Report, _Bright Words_, Edinburgh, November 1938.

18. _Stornoway Gazette and West Coast Advertiser_, 26 January, 1951.

19. W. C. MacKenzie, _The Western Isles: Their History, Traditions and Place Names_, Paisley: A. Gardner Ltd, 1932, pp. 63–67.

20. Bryan R. Wilson, 'An Analysis of Sect Development', _American Sociological Review_ 24.1, 1959, pp. 3–15.

21. E.g., the Salvation Army, see Robertson, _op. cit._, p. 105.

22. In contrast to many conversionist groups which began with ecumenical counter-sectarian pretensions but frequently developed into sects. This point is illustrated more fully in Wilson, _Patterns of Sectarianism_, pp. 20 and 120.

23. G. Lenski, _The Religious Factor_, New York: Doubleday, 1961, esp. pp. 115–125.

24. The Keswick Convention was for these reasons excluded from an account of Holiness movements in mid-twentieth century Britain. J. Ford, _What the Holiness People Believe_, London: Barker, 1954. See also J. Ford, _The Church of the Nazarene in Britain, The International Holiness Mission and The Calvary Holiness Church, with special reference to Holiness movements in Christian history_. Ph.D. thesis, University of London, 1967.

25. D. A Martin, 'The Denomination', _British Journal of Sociology_, 13.1, pp. 1–14, reprinted in _Pacifism_, London: Routledge and Kegan Paul, 1965, pp. 208–24.

26. See Orr, _op. cit._, ch. 5, and F. M. Davenport, _Primitive Traits in Religious Revivals_, London: Macmillan, 1905, Ch. 7.

27. Bryan R. Wilson, _Sects and Society_, London: Heinemann, 1961, p. 98.

28. Orr, _op. cit._, p. 41.

29. James G. Leyburn, _The Scotch-Irish_, Chapel Hill: University of North Carolina Press, 1962, pp. 278–9.

30. Warburton, _op. cit._, p. 141; Wilson, _Sects and Society_, p. 102.

31. There is an affiliated but independent mission in France (La Mission de Foi Evangile) which was founded by two ex-pilgrims but it has almost no role in the affairs of the Faith Mission except in making use of some of the College graduates.

5   Religious Conflict in Northern Ireland

Robin Jenkins

SOON after it was announced that the Archbishop of Canterbury might visit the Pope, the following letter from the general secretary of the Christian Fellowship Centre was published in the *Belfast News-Letter*:

> We desire to place on record our deep dismay and sorrow at the proposed visit to the Pope by his Grace, The Archbishop of Canterbury. This is indeed a grievous blow to our evangelical position, and a step that will inevitably draw the judgement of God on Church and State. We would call upon Christian people in all our Churches to devote themselves increasingly to prayer. We need delude ourselves no longer. The die is cast—the step has been taken. The most we can do now is to pray for courage and faith, that we might be true to the simplicity of the gospel in this dark hour and the darker days that lie before us. We respectfully suggest that in those Churches and Mission Halls where evangelical truth is still cherished, the National Anthem should be sung as a prayer next Sunday, with the congregation and minister kneeling in the attitude of prayer.[1]

When many Protestants confine the term 'Christian' to those who can claim the conscious experience of a moment of salvation, and a large number of Catholics believe the Protestant faith to be anathema, it is hardly surprising that views such as those above get expression in the mass media. If the religious conflict simply amounted to a conflict of ideas, life in Northern Ireland might be quite invigorating; in fact the conflict is of ontological proportions and, as a consequence, life is poisoned by an atmosphere of distrust, discrimination, plotting and hate.

Historically, the conflict can be traced back to 1171 when Henry II invaded Ireland; most of what has happened in Ireland since then has increased the differences between the original inhabitants and the English settlers. Thus, in 1366, the Statutes of Kilkenny attempted to prevent the two groups from mixing and this had the effect of separating the English from the Irish clergy in the Church. In 1541, Henry VIII had himself crowned King of Ireland, making the differences yet greater. In 1641 the Irish rebelled against the colonists and massacred many Protestants and in 1649 Cromwell massacred many

Catholics. In 1690 the Catholic James II, who had fled to Ireland in 1689, was decisively defeated by the Protestant William III in the Battle of the Boyne. In 1798 the Irish organized a rebellion that failed, partly because of the strength of the Orange Orders, which had been formed a few years previously. The 1845 potato famine, the 1916 uprising and the 1920 Government of Ireland Act only served to widen the gap between the two communities.

Any attempt to interpret these events must inevitably be partisan. Ireland has two histories – one for each religious community. This is reflected in their language, their slogans and their interpretations of the present. History weighs heavily when wall slogans include – 'Remember 1690', 'No surrender', and '1916.' It would be difficult to overestimate the degree to which these dates impinge on the present, arise in arguments and become justifications for present activities. The people of Northern Ireland were born into a conflict, each day of their lives they are reminded of it, and there is no reason to believe that the situation will change radically during their lifetime.

It is frequently claimed that things are getting better, that the conflict is far less intense than it was twenty years ago, that the Rev. Ian Paisley's activities are a backlash symptom of increasing accord. This opinion requires careful examination for it has the flavour of wishful thinking and perhaps even sympathetic magic – the hope certainly exists that the more it is said that there is increasing accord, the more likely it is to be true.

The following is a short examination of the evidence that is available – and the words 'is available' are intentional, because the situation is such that important evidence is not easy to come by.

The population of Northern Ireland is just one and a half million; half a million are Catholics and the rest are Protestants. In the 1961 census, less than 30,000 people failed to state a religion; 413,000 were Presbyterians, 413,000 were Church of Ireland and 345,000 were Methodists; the other Protestant sects number 70,000 members in all. As can be seen from the map, all groups are not evenly distributed throughout Northern Ireland. The area around Belfast is over 75% Protestant and the areas along the frontier with Eire are over 75% Catholic. Large areas and many of the towns have proportions 40 to 60 either way.

Religion and politics in Northern Ireland have been inextricably mixed since the reign of Henry VIII. It follows that in a society

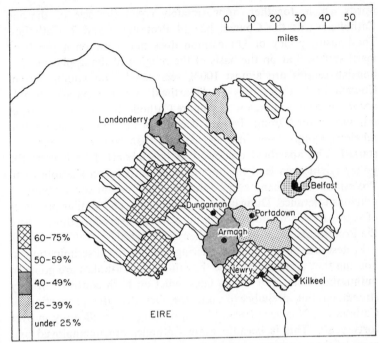

Percentage of Roman Catholics in 1951[2]

which holds to the formal notion of 'one man, one vote' the relation between politics and religion should vary according to the proportions of the two religious groups. In general all Unionists (Conservatives) are Protestant. A few Protestants vote Liberal or Labour; so do some Catholics, but both of these parties are very small. A large number of Catholics do not vote (since voting is seen as giving legitimacy to the establishment of Ulster as part of Britain), and the rest vote Republican, National Unity or Republican Labour. The Unionist government has not been touched by any of the other parties for over forty years; to make sure that this continues, most elections are gerrymandered in favour of the Unionists at both the national and local levels.

In a few towns with large Catholic majorities, like Newry, the Catholics do in fact control the town council; in other towns with similar Catholic majorities, like Londonderry, the Protestants have political control. The gerrymander comes out clearly in towns that are near to the 50–50 mix. Dungannon, for instance, which is 53% Catholic, is divided into three electoral wards – two Protestant wards which, together, approximately equal the size of the one Catholic ward; the Council has 14 Protestants and 7 Catholics. The housing policy of Dungannon does not work on a points or merit system, but on the basis of the religion of the applicant. The housing estates are almost 100% segregated. Dungannon Urban Council in fact practises an 'apartheid' which separates people according to their religion. If you are Catholic, it is impossible to get a house on the 'Orange Estate'. Because of this separation, the two religious groups come into less contact than before the rehousing started. The apartheid analogy can be elaborated at length; the policy might even lead to short term peace between Catholics and Protestants but it can never be the basis of a decent society built on religious tolerance. Dungannon is not unusual and similar processes of segregation are under way in most towns, especially those where the Protestants have their supremacy threatened.[3]

Protestants justify gerrymandering and all the discrimination in housing that it entails because they think the Catholics are going to outnumber them. The Pope's latest edict on birth control will only strengthen this prejudice despite the fact that the proportion of Catholics in Northern Ireland has not changed significantly in over forty years. This is because more Catholics are unemployed and more of them emigrate, proportionately, than Protestants.

In the rest of Britain, religion has long ceased to influence people's secular expectations, but in Northern Ireland, religion affects most areas of life. It determines the school children go to, the part of the town their parents live in, the sort of job their parents have. In short, religion determines life expectations.

A child in Northern Ireland is unlikely to play with children of the other religion simply because the housing policy of most town councils does not mix the religious groups. After the age of five, however, the separation becomes formal because almost no children go to religiously mixed schools. The history of this segregation is complex and like all other aspects of the history of Northern Ireland, lends itself to two interpretations. Catholics refuse to hand over their church-financed schools to the state because they fear interference with the teaching of religion by a state education system that is to all intents Protestant. On the other side, the state refuses to finance Catholic schools because they refuse to integrate with the state system which is formally independent of religion. Whether the state education system is a secular or a religious system is therefore part of the controversy. Only in institutions for higher education is there any mixing of religions, though even here there is the notable exception of teacher-training colleges.

On leaving school, discrimination takes over from segregation. Although advertisements for jobs rarely state religious requirements there is no doubt that discrimination is part of the hiring and firing policy of most organizations. There are of course numerous individual reports of discrimination that are difficult to prove but in many branches of employment the gross statistics tell their own tale. The Northern Ireland Housing Trust, National Assistance Board, General Health Services Board and Economic Council, have a total of 52 members on their boards; not one of them is Catholic. Over 94 per cent of the Civil Service of Northern Ireland is Protestant, and in local government the discrimination is probably even worse. Councillors often take it for granted that they should dispense patronage to their own side and applicants for public appointments expect to canvas Councillors personally. Among private firms the situation varies: in some there is complete discrimination; in others internal discrimination over status; in yet others – a small minority – employees are deliberately mixed.

A similar picture emerges from an analysis of voluntary associations; almost all of them are divided by religion. Catholics meet Catholics in one place, and Protestants meet Protestants in another. They live in different parts of the town, send their children to different schools, worship in different churches and even play different types of football. Religion and politics and social relations are inseparable; consequently they divide the people again and again.

This is the basic problem in Northern Ireland – that religion expresses the polarization of the community into two groups. A succession of historical events has made it that way and a lot more will have to happen before much changes. In England, politics and religion and social relations have never been so intertwined; Conservatives might equally well be Protestant or Catholic and Protestants vote Labour and Conservative. This criss-cross of conflicts creates a pattern of divided loyalties that sews the system together. In Northern Ireland there is no such criss-cross and the divide made by religion is widened by politics which in turn is widened by the whole web of group affiliations. All this conflict takes place within the context of an ongoing debate about ecumenical unification. Consequently there is a growing rift between the clergy, who are becoming more gradualist and more compromising in their attitudes towards the conflict, and the laity, many of whom retain their old absolutist attitudes, so well expressed in the letter quoted earlier. Although the Prime Minister, Captain O'Neill, favours increased co-operation with Eire, he does not even carry a majority of his own supporters with him. Although the dignitaries of the Church of Ireland are in favour of the eventual re-unification of the Catholic and Protestant branches of the Church, only a minority of Church of Ireland laity agrees. Generally speaking, attitudes are more extreme in towns where neither Protestant nor Catholic is clearly completely dominant, where, as a consequence, either group could conceivably be dominant were it not for the gerrymander. It was in some of these towns that Ian Paisley was polarizing the situation before he was sent to prison for three months in 1965. As ecumenical unification comes nearer it is possible to predict more strain and conflict *within* both the Protestant and Catholic Churches in Northern Ireland, in addition to the conflict between the Protestants and Catholics.

It is difficult to be optimistic for the future because so many aspects of the present situation constitute parts of a vicious circle. There is no obvious way of breaking this circle and there is no point in making pious remarks about tolerance between religions and loving your neighbour. In the absence of any solution, many people seem to believe that things will indeed get better if they say that they are often enough. But this is no solution either. Whatever happens, though, the conflict is unlikely to be resolved in London or Rome because it is not just a matter of conflicting beliefs, both of which appear to be rational beliefs to the believers, but a question of something embedded very deep in the culture of Northern Ireland. Perhaps the conflict will only cease when the culture has become indifferent to religion.

NOTES

1. The *Belfast News-Letter*, 4 November 1960, quoted by D. P. Barritt and C. F. Carter, *The Northern Ireland Problem*, London: Oxford University Press, 1962, p. 25.

2. Reproduced from the article by Emrys Jones, 'Problems of Partition and Segregation in Northern Ireland', *Journal of Conflict Resolution* 4.1, Ann Arbor, 1960, p. 98.

3. R. Jenkins and J. MacRae, 'Religion, Conflict and Polarization in Northern Ireland), in *Studies in Peace Research* I, ed. B. Röling, Assen: Royal Van Goreum, 1968.

6 Puritan and Antipuritan: Types of Vocation to the Ordained Ministry[1]

Robert Towler

CONSIDERABLE attention has been devoted to the clergy in recent sociological literature. The priest or minister's function in the various denominations, and his relationship to the wider society, have been discussed at length. However, the training for the ministry has been the subject of only a few investigations. The study on which this paper is based was started in 1965 and aims to help fill this gap in research. Of the twenty-five theological colleges of the Anglican Church in England, five were selected to be as representative as possible. Their total intake for the year 1966 was interviewed either before entering the colleges or shortly after arrival, and has been interviewed at six-monthly intervals since.[2]

A thorough basic grounding in theology is the formal end of the course provided by a theological college, but of course the training involves a great deal more. As a prerequisite to the analysis of occupational socialization – by which is meant the complex changes in attitudes, values and ideas to those typical of the occupational subculture which take place as part of the 'formation' of a clergy-man – it is necessary to distinguish the differences among candidates for the ministry at the beginning of training. Only in the light of such differences can subsequent changes be studied and accurately interpreted as aspects of the socialization of ordinands.

Some differences among Anglican ordinands are obvious. There are wide differences in age and in level of educational achievement for instance. Other differences, like those of churchmanship, are less readily described since they depend upon a combination of factors. It is just such complex differences which are of interest. The extent of these differences is such that it is more useful to speak of different kinds of vocation to the ordained ministry than simply of differences among ordinands. Richard Niebuhr has delineated types of vocation in terms of the balance between four elements in the definition of a call to the ministry.[3] James Gustafson has distinguished a number of motivational types of vocation.[4] Both pieces of work are American, however, and not immediately applicable to the circumstances of religion in Britain. What is needed is an analysis of the British situation in terms relevant to an empirical discussion rather than a theological or psychodynamic one.

PROCEDURE AND RESULTS

In the present study established scales were used to obtain quantitative assessments of respondents on a number of behavioural variables. The six scales of the British version of the Allport-Vernon-Lindzey *Study of Values* were used, together with the three scales of the *Eysenck Personality Inventory*, and four scales, slightly adapted for use with British subjects, of the *Theological School Inventory*.[5] On the basis of the results of these tests it was hoped to be able to distinguish types of vocation to the ministry which would be meaningful in relation to established distinctions, such as churchmanship, but which would have been derived independently.

The respondents' scores on twelve of thirteen variables being used were subjected to a factor analysis, and one factor alone emerged which was both significant and meaningful.[6] Five of the twelve variables had high loadings on this factor, and since space permits no more than a brief description of the results, the discussion will be limited to these five variables.

1. *Religious interest*   A high score on this scale from the Study of Values indicates a great importance attached to religious matters. It measures the extent to which participation in traditional religious institutions helps an individual to find a meaning in life and see all experience as a meaningful whole.[7]

2. *Aesthetic interest*   This scale, from the same test, assesses the degree to which a person judges beauty and harmony of greater importance than truth or utility. The respondent who scores high on this variable tends to be an individualist, and is interested in other people for their own sake rather than concerned with their well-being.

Because of the structure of the Study of Values these two variables are not independent, and this is a serious disadvantage of the test. However, there is reason to suppose that the interdependence of these two variables does not invalidate their inclusion in a preliminary correlation analysis here.[8]

3. *Special leadings* This variable, from the Theological School Inventory, focuses on the extent to which a respondent defines his own occupational choice of the ministry in terms of a response to a supernatural directive rather than as a reasoned decision. In the words of one item on this scale, 'I answered a call more compelling than any rational assessment.'

4. *Concept of the call* From the same test, this variable indicates the extent to which a respondent believes a supernatural type of call to be normative and necessary. It is concerned with the same thing as the 'special leadings' variable, but measures the respondent's concept of vocation rather than his experience of it.

5. *Flexibility* The fifth variable, also from the Theological School Inventory, measures the level of an individual's tolerance of ambiguity, doubt or change, especially in the area of attitudes and beliefs. It is the inverse of the more common type of rigidity or dogmatism scales.[9]

All these five variables had high loadings on the single factor being considered. Of the whole group of respondents, 60% had significantly high scores on this factor, which was made up of 30% who had high positive scores and 30% who had high negative scores. The remaining 40% of respondents had insignificant scores on this factor and will not be discussed. Only the 60% are considered here. The respondents with high positive scores on this factor had high scores on the 'religious interest', 'special leadings' and 'concept of the call' variables, and low scores on the 'aesthetic interest' and 'flexibility' variables. The other group of respondents, who had high negative scores on this factor, had, conversely, high scores on 'aesthetic interest' and 'flexibility', and low scores on 'religious interest', 'special leadings', and 'concept of the call'. These two groups emerged, polarized by a single factor. They will be considered to constitute two opposite types of vocation.

DISCUSSION

In the initial stages of the study a certain broad variation was intuitively observed among the religious interests of the respondents.

To put it crudely – for it was originally perceived crudely – some respondents seemed more religious than others. This observation was made from informal conversations. Some respondents seemed to be interested in religion to the exclusion of all else. There was a tendency to talk about matters quite unconnected with religion within a religious frame of reference. Religion seemed to be the major referent for all matters of interest, and subjects of conversation which could not be fitted into the religious frame of reference were quite noticeably avoided. On the other hand there were those who talked about everything but religion. Most often they spoke of their interest in the arts, which was one topic hardly ever mentioned by the more religious individuals. The attitudes to specifically religious activities, like prayer, preaching and church services, were also in sharp contrast. For the majority of ordinands studied, attitudes to their cultic activities could best be described as casual. But this was notably not the case with those who appeared more religious. Their attitude was, rather, serious and zealous, and they seemed to derive conscious satisfaction and pleasure from these activities.

These intuitive observations were corroborated by the empirical findings, for two groups emerged: the one religious and the other unreligious. Since by virtue of their occupational choice all the respondents must be viewed as religious, in some sense or other, what is at variance is the type of religiousness. The two kinds of religiousness or types of vocation which emerged will be called *puritan* and *antipuritan* for convenience. These designations are not entirely satisfactory, but they make discussion easier than it would be if one spoke of X and Y types of vocation, and they have a certain descriptive usefulness. The *puritan* type of vocation is characterized in the first place by a high degree of religious interest combined with low flexibility. This implies an overwhelming interest in religious matters to the practical exclusion of all else. Furthermore, the low flexibility score, which is equivalent to a high dogmatism score, implies a total and uncompromising commitment to religious beliefs and values. This is the sort of faith which is clearly defined, rigidly maintained, and completely dominant within an individual's system of beliefs and values. In the second place the puritan vocation type is characterized by high scores on special leadings and concept of the call. This means that the individual has a strong sense of having been singled out by God to receive a personal and immediate call to enter the full-time ministry. To this extent he believes he has a special qualification for being ordained, and that his vocation is above challenge or discussion by other people. In addition he believes that only those who have his sense of divine calling should be ordained. The individual with a puritan type of vocation is not only sure of his personal calling, but also convinced that it is the only valid ground for entering the ordained ministry.

Finally the puritan type of vocation is characterized by a low score on the aesthetic interest variable. The obvious implication is that the typical puritan has not time for the arts since they only divert attention from religion, which is of supreme importance. But aesthetic interests are often rejected as part of an indifference or aversion to the cultural values of secular society. This is a more satisfactory explanation of the extremely low scores on aesthetic interest which characterize those with a puritan type of vocation. All these characteristics fit together to form a coherent whole, which is dominated by the sense of the supernatural. The overwhelming experience of having received a divine call to the ministry, which is usually accompanied by some sort of conversion experience, gives ample grounds on which a clearly defined set of religious beliefs and values can be maintained. They are based not on their reasonableness but on what is defined as a personal experience of their supernatural revelation. Just as a puritan feels compelled in his choice of the ministry as an occupation, so he feels a compulsion to accept his religious beliefs. Similarly the strong sense of the supernatural leads to certain attitudes towards the non-religious aspects of life. Great importance is attached to religious and other-worldly values at the expense of this-worldly values, and hence the lack of interest in the arts. A certain withdrawal from the world and aversion to the cultural values of secular society is a natural corollary of the puritan's strong sense of the supernatural. This, then, is a brief picture of the puritan type of vocation.

A particularly religious sort of ordinand was observed intuitively. This was substantiated empirically and a more detailed picture of this type of vocation could be gained. The same is true of the notably unreligious sort of ordinand who also was observed intuitively. The *antipuritan* type of vocation is characterized, first, by a low degree of religious interest, compared with the average for all ordinands tested. The mean antipuritan score on this variable is not greatly higher than that for the general population.[10] This, combined with a high flexibility score, suggests a type of commitment to religious beliefs which leaves much room for other interests, and considerable openness to doubt about the religious beliefs themselves. Religion may be important for the individual with this type of vocation – it clearly is, from the occupational choice of the ministry – but it is only one interest among a number which he finds important, and while he may hold a set of religious beliefs and values with whole-hearted conviction, they are not maintained dogmatically.

Secondly, the antipuritan type of vocation has characteristically low scores on special leadings and concept of the call. In other words the antipuritan sort of ordinand sees his vocation to the ministry as a reasonable choice of the job he is best fitted for by his temperament, abilities and training. Within the context of his religious faith, he views it as the best contribution he can make to the work of the Church, both in his own judgement and in that of the representatives of the Church responsible for selecting future clergy. The decision is not seen as an answer to a direct call from God in any sense which would not be equally true of the decision to get married or go into the Civil Service. While the antipuritan type of ordinand may recognize that other people have a sense of divine call, he sees such a sense as in no way a *sine qua non* for ordination, as does his puritan counterpart.

Thirdly, the antipuritan type of vocation is characterized by a high score on aesthetic interest. An interest in the arts generally, or in some particular field of the arts, invariably accompanies the relatively low interest in religion and other characteristics which have been mentioned. In contrast to the puritan, the antipuritan does not conceive religion as being opposed to secular interests and values. On the contrary, he frequently finds in the arts and non-religious affairs more interest and 'inspiration' than he does in religion. Perhaps it is because of the current vogue of the writings of J. R. R. Tolkien, but more than one respondent remarked quite spontaneously that he found more inspiration in *The Lord of the Rings* than in the Bible. Others discussed Antonioni, Marx or J. S. Bach with the same fervour that puritan ordinands devoted to a text from the Bible, or the writings of St Thomas Aquinas or Paul Tillich. The characteristics of the antipuritan type of vocation, too, form a coherent whole. Just as the puritan type is dominated by a personal experience of God and a sense of contact with a transcendent super-natural, so the antipuritan vocation is dominated by a lack of concern with any specifically religious interests and with a search for religious meaning within the realm of natural experience. The lack of any compelling experience of the supernatural means that his religious beliefs are maintained with only the same degree of certainty as is his occupational choice. The decision to enter the ministry is made either rationally or sometimes casually, as a natural step in a series of decisions, but never as the result of a feeling of overwhelming compulsion. So the religious beliefs of the antipuritan ordinand are held by choice or as the natural development of his thought. They are never the result of a sudden conversion or feeling of compulsion. Interest in the arts and involvement in secular culture are logical within the context of an antipuritan type of vocation. Since there is no sense of alienation between the religious and secular spheres, but rather religious beliefs and the decision to be ordained occur naturally, the search for further religious meaning immanent within the secular sphere is quite natural.[11]

These two types of vocation to the ministry are by no means exhaustive. 40% of the ordinands studied fit into neither category; they are a mixture of the two types or unclassifiable in these terms. It is nevertheless surprising that two such clearly delineated types of vocation should account for as high a proportion as 60% of the group which was being studied. The question immediately arises as to the relation of the distinction between the puritan and antipuritan vocation types to other more obvious distinctions. It was found, on the one hand, that there is no relationship whatever to the age of the respondents. Nor is there any correlation between types of vocation and the sociologically important dichotomy of normal and late vocational choices.[12] The two types of vocation are found equally among ordinands of all ages and among those who have been in previous occupations and those who have not. Again there is no relationship to respondents' levels of educational achievement or to the type of education they received. On the other hand, a relationship was found between types of vocation and the complex distinctions which constitute the 'churchmanship' of respondents.

This relationship must be considered under three headings to avoid unnecessary confusion. In the first place we deal with churchmanship simply in terms of the respondents' own self-definitions. They defined themselves broadly as either catholics, evangelicals or modernists.[13] For the most part, those with a puritan type of vocation defined themselves as evangelicals, though not exclusively so. Respondents of the antipuritan vocation type were split almost equally between those who defined themselves as catholics and those who defined themselves as modernists. The presence among the antipuritans (who can be seen to be religiously liberal rather than conservative) of those who, during their training, refer to themselves as catholics is of particular interest in the light of certain points raised by Michael Daniel in the last edition of this *Yearbook*.[14]

In the second place, a relationship was found between vocation type and what respondents perceived as the primary role of the contemporary clergyman. Since these perceptions are closely associated with churchmanship they must be considered as another aspect of it. It would be misleading to treat them as independent. Those with a puritan type of vocation conceive the ministry primarily in terms of preaching. For them, the first duty of the clergyman is as a preacher of 'the Word of God'. This is to be expected from the predominance of evangelicals among those with a puritan type of vocation. Of the antipuritans, however, some see the clergyman's role as primarily that of a pastor, while others perceive it mainly as a liturgical or sacerdotal role. Again, this is in keeping with the presence among the antipuritans of those with both catholic and modernist self-definitions.

A third distinction which is associated with churchmanship bears a significant relationship to types of vocation. This is the attitude of respondents on questions of sexual morality. Using the very simple criterion of whether or not sexual relations outside marriage, including fornication, adultery and homosexual relations, are thought to be always wrong, it was found that the great majority of those with a puritan type of vocation maintained that they always are. Most respondents of the antipuritan type, however, did not think so. This finding is consistent with the different mean scores of the two groups on the flexibility variable. The puritan dogmatically maintains that sexual relations outside marriage are always wrong, whereas the antipuritan is less definite and more flexible in his attitude.[15]

Although variation in attitudes on sexual morality has been considered under the heading of churchmanship, its implications are rather wider. Strict views on sexual morality are certainly indicative, in the context of the present study, of a dogmatically conservative and puritanical religious orientation, but they also imply certain broader social attitudes. The person who maintains strict moral views is often found to be strongly aware of the expectations of others. In a religious context the relevant others may be either a postulated supernatural other, whose authority has been seen to dominate the *Weltanschauung* of the typical puritan, or the other members of the religious group, or both. The results of one variable not included in the factor analysis are relevant here. This variable is the 'lie scale' of the Eysenck Personality Inventory.[16] As the name implies, the main purpose of the scale is to estimate the reliability of respondents' answers to questions in general, but high scores on the lie scale are of interest in themselves. It consists of eight items for which a certain response is highly probable. Thus the answers to such questions as, for instance, 'As a child, did you always do as you were told immediately and without grumbling?' and, 'Have you sometimes told lies in your life?' are highly predictable for most people. When an individual gives more than one or two highly improbable answers the implication may be that, rather than being a generally unreliable respondent, he has a strong tendency to answer certain moral questions in a way which conforms to the strictest expectations of relevant others. We are reminded of the Victorian Naval Officer who 'never – well hardly ever – used a big big D——'. Bearing out the second interpretation of strict views on sexual morality, it was found that high lie scores were significantly associated with strict moral attitudes. Of course this is based on the assumption that a high lie score, rather than simply casting doubt on the veracity of an individual's responses, does indicate a heightened awareness of the expectations others have of him, and a more powerful desire to conform to the expectations of relevant others than to tell the truth.[17]

Having described the two distinct types of vocation to the ministry which emerged from this study of a group of Anglican ordinands, a similarity may be observed between the puritan vocation type and a certain other religious orientation. This will lead on to an interpretation of the two types of vocation. In a paper which has already become a classic in the sociology of religion, Bryan Wilson characterizes the sect, and draws out the distinction between a denomination and a sect with a clarity rarely achieved by others writing about religious organizations.[18] Going on from Weber and Troeltsch as well as more recent writers, he argues that the member of a sectarian organization has a characteristic type of religious commitment:

. . . although sects differ among themselves in their characteristic social relationships, the commitment of the sectarian is always more total and more defined than that of the member of other religious organizations. The ideology

of the sect is much more clearly crystallized and the member is much more
distinctly characterized than is the adherent of the larger denomination or
church. The behavioural correlates of his ideological commitment also serve
to set him and keep him apart from 'the world'.[19]

From this passage and from elsewhere in the same paper, there is a
readily recognizable similarity between the type of religious commitment which characterizes the sectarian and that which has been
described for the ordinand with a puritan type of vocation. Space
does not permit the several similarities to be spelt out, but they are
not in any case hard for anyone familiar with Wilson's paper to see.
What is important is that in his total rather than segmental commitment to a set of religious beliefs and values, which are held in
sharp contrast to those of secular society, the puritan ordinand is
similar in kind to the sectarian. The difference in degree is largely
the result of not belonging, at least primarily, to an organization
which incorporates these attitudes and articulates them in an institutionalized way. But it should be noted that within an organization
such as the Church of England, which more closely resembles an
ecclesia than a *denomination* in Milton Yinger's terms, sectarian
organizations are accommodated with little difficulty or serious
dysfunction.[20] These do provide institutionalized opportunities for
the articulation and reinforcement of sectarian tendencies. The
Inter-Varsity Fellowship may be taken as an example of an organization which is constituted of persons who are largely members, and
often clergymen, of the Church of England, and yet which is, to use
Wilson's words characterizing the Conversionist sect:

. . . distrustful of, or indifferent towards, the denominations and churches
which have at best diluted, at worst betrayed, Christianity . . .[21]

Both the sectarian and the puritan type of ordinand, then, have
this total commitment to religious beliefs and values. The consequence of this sociological fact is that the individual has a single,
religious frame of reference, which is at the root of the socio-
psychological characteristics which have been seen to typify the
puritan ordinand. It is total religious commitment which contrasts
the sectarian with the member of a denomination; and it is total
commitment which contrasts the puritan ordinand with both the
average member of his church and also most of his fellow-ordinands,
who are only segmentally committed to the religious organization
and its beliefs.

It may appear, in the light of what has been said of the puritan type of vocation, that the antipuritan type is simply less religious. After all, the lower degree of religious interest of the average antipuritan has been stressed. Perhaps the typical antipuritan has only segmental commitment to religion, which would be characteristically denominational. I do not think so. It is merely anomalous that while the puritan and antipuritan are more and less religious ideologically, in behavioural terms their commitment is equal. Both are training for the full-time ministry. I would argue that the two types share one essential element, which is their common rejection of the segmental commitment characteristic of the denomination. We have seen how this is effected for the puritan; the antipuritan finds a total religious frame of reference unacceptable, and having rejected many of the institutionalized beliefs and values, he tries to find a total commitment to a set of beliefs and values outside the organization, within secular society. A vocation to the full-time ministry necessarily implies total, or nearly total commitment to the religious organization. And both types of vocation, in contrast to the partial commitment of the denomination, assert a total religious commitment: the difference is that the one does so in the religious context, and the other seeks to do so outside it.

It remains only to examine briefly the broader implications of the two types of vocation and to place them in a meaningful perspective of historical developments and the general situation of the present day. First, is the phenomenon of these two completely antipathetic types new? The puritan type certainly is not new: it is a reassertion of the traditional Protestant position. Nor is such a movement within the Church of England without ample precedent.

The antipuritan type, however, is a different matter. In the first place it is unlike either the catholic or the modernist tradition, since respondents of the antipuritan type come equally from each. It is new in that it seems to be trying to affirm, not the traditional Christian beliefs in new terms or a novel way, but secular beliefs and values in the name of the Christian faith whose traditional teachings are consistently and self-consciously doubted. This, it seems, is new. It represents a form of radicalism which could hardly become more extreme in a modal form such as this is. Despite its extremeness and lack of apparent internal logic, it is a logical development of some recent trends. The movement for religionless Christianity and a demythologized faith has taught a new generation of ordinands to take fairly lightly assertions of historical fact, clearly defined doctrine and simple moral codes. When, with such a background of attenuated religious beliefs, ordinands try to identify themselves completely with secular values and non-religious causes within a differentiated society, in which privatized religion and denominational pluralism are basic religious assumptions, the result is bound to be confusing, if not confused.

Much of the foregoing discussion has been devoted to psychological rather than sociological considerations. Most of the distinctions drawn between the two vocation types are indeed psychological; they are types of individual differences within an institutionalized church. The important point, however, is that the present divergence between puritan and antipuritan types of vocation, between conservatives and radicals, does not derive from such internal disputes as gave rise to the split between high churchmen and low churchmen. It is a sociological phenomenon in which theological issues are secondary. The conservatives and radicals represent different responses of religious belief to the external forces of secularism. It is the confrontation with contemporary western society, which is by definition secular, that has evoked the polarized religious responses represented by these two types of vocation to the ordained ministry. Miss Monica Furlong's recent perceptive comment on the split in the Roman Catholic Church is extremely pertinent:

> The real divide between the conservatives and radicals lies in external questions. . . . Both conservative and radical appear guilty of an attempt to 'turn the Church on'—the one side by strenuous reorganization, the other by a frenzied social activism. The conservative does not care to notice that his efforts have become meaningless to the outside world. The radical often appears content to settle for a humanist society in which the Christian resolves his conflicts by concentrating on his relationship with his neighbour, and omitting the talk about God.[22]

So although the variables which have been discussed have been socio-psychological, the context in which they appear, and the situation which has given rise to the dichotomous pattern which has been described, are sociological.

It is suggested, then, that the two types of vocation found among ordinands in this study represent two distinct responses of 'religion in secular society'. Neither is a denominational response in so far as neither accepts the partial role of religion which is the hall-mark of denominational religion in a differentiated society. Each seeks a single and total frame of reference. To this end the puritan retreats from the secular and asserts again total commitment to conversionist, personalized, otherworldly, religious beliefs and values in the religious subculture. The antipuritan accepts the secular and, on the basis of what he perceives as demythologized and religionless Christianity, seeks to find and express his religious faith in a secular context.

NOTES

1. Based on a section of the author's Ph.D. thesis, *An Analysis of the Professional Socialization of Anglican Ordinands* (Leeds, in progress).
2. The actual number interviewed was 80.
3. H. R. Niebuhr, *The Purpose of the Church and its Ministry*, New York: Harper and Brothers, 1956, pp. 64ff.
4. J. M. Gustafson in H. R. Niebuhr, D. D. Williams and J. M. Gustafson (eds.), *The Advancement of Theological Education*, New York: Harper and Brothers, 1957, pp. 146ff.
5. For details of these tests see the appropriate manuals: S. Richardson, *Manual for Study of Values*, Slough: The National Foundation for Educational Research, 1965; H. J. Eysenck and S. B. G. Eysenck, *Manual of the Eysenck Personality Inventory*, London: University of London Press, 1964; J. E. Dittes, *Vocational Guidance of Theological Students*, Dayton, Ohio: Ministry Studies Board, 1964.
6. The factor accounts for only 25.6 per cent of the total variance. However, five variables load highly onto it, and each of the other five factors with a latent root greater than unity, accounting for about 10 per cent of the variance each, has only one or two high loadings. Considering that the Varimax method of factor rotation was used, which is designed to preclude the generation of a 'general' factor, the result is the more significant.
7. The manuals of both the American and British versions of the Study of Values claim that this scale measures a general religious interest. R. A. Hunt has argued that it measures a more limited and specific field of interest. The evidence he presents is very convincing, and it substantiates the criticism which was made originally by Donald Super. Cf. R. A. Hunt, 'The Interpretation of the Religious Scale of the Allport-Vernon-Lindzey Study of Values', *Journal for the Scientific Study of Religion* 6, 1968, pp. 65–77; D. E. Super, *Appraising Vocational Fitness*, New York: Harper, 1949.
8. With a mixed group of respondents, a correlation of —0.23 was found (Richardson, *op. cit.*, p. 16), whereas it was —0.53 for the present group. The difference is sufficient to justify further consideration.
9. Perhaps the nearest equivalent to this is Milton Rokeach's Dogmatism Scale. Neither is subject to the same limitations as either the California F Scale, which is biased to right-wing authoritarianism, or the Gough-Stanford Rigidity Scale, which is biased to those with particular abilities in analytic thinking. It is worth observing that Rokeach's work should be of importance in future studies of religious beliefs. Cf. M. Rokeach, *The Open and Closed Mind*, New York: Basic Books, 1960.
10. For the religious interest scale of the Study of Values, the mean score for a sample of the general population was 27.2 (cf. Richardson, *op. cit.*); for anti-

puritans, 34.1; for the whole group of ordinands tested, 42.9; and for the puritans, 51.4.

11. For a sociological account of the Reformation which is relevant as a background to distinction between puritan and antipuritan types of vocation, see G. E. Swanson, *Religion and Regime*, Ann Arbor: University of Michigan Press, 1967.

12. Cf. A. P. M. Coxon, 'Patterns of Occupational Recruitment: The Anglican Ministry', *Sociology* 1, 1967, pp. 73–79.

13. These categories are sometimes said to be obsolete, but respondents had little difficulty in defining themselves in these terms. Only to those who came from overseas provinces of the Anglican Communion were the terms not meaningful.

14. M. Daniel, 'Catholic, Evangelical and Liberal', *op. cit.*, pp. 115–23.

15. The relationships between vocation types and all three of the above distinctions are significant beyond the 0.001 level of probability, using the chi-square test for significance on the null hypotheses. This is an appropriate test since N is only 20 or thereabouts.

16. It may be noted that the two scales of this personality test did not prove to be significant in isolating types of vocation. This is consistent with other research findings. See, for instance, L. B. Brown, 'The Structure of Religious Beliefs', *Journal for the Scientific Study of Religion* 5, 1966, pp. 259–272.

17. Cf. S. B. G. Eysenck and H. J. Eysenck, 'An Experimental Investigation of Desirability Response Set in a Personality Questionnaire', *Life Sciences*, 1963, No. 5, pp. 343–355.

18. B. R. Wilson, 'An Analysis of Sect Development', *American Sociological Review*, 24.1, 1959, pp. 3–15.

19. *Op. cit.*, p. 4.

20. Cf. J. M. Yinger, *Religion, Society and the Individual*, New York: Macmillan, 1957, pp. 147ff.

21. Wilson, *op. cit.*, p. 6.

22. An article in *The Sunday Times*, 4 August 1968.

7 Nineteenth-century Urbanization and Religion: Bristol and Marseilles 1830-1880

R. Martin Goodridge

Introduction

It is noteworthy that the founding fathers of the sociology of religion – Max Weber, Ernst Troeltsch and Emile Durkheim – were all largely concerned with the historical aspects of the sociology of religion. Equally noteworthy is the fact that most British sociologists interested in religion have been and are concerned with contemporary matters, sometimes for reasons of pastoral concern or ecclesiastical administration.

However it is strongly felt that such an approach in sociology, particularly with regard to the religious specialism, is highly dangerous and can lead to much erroneous interpretation of current trends and situations. As David Martin has pointed out:

> The first need in Britain is for research to find out what has happened historically.[1]

This view of the importance of history has been developed and strengthened in this author as he has pursued his research on religious practice in Bristol and Marseilles in the mid-nineteenth century. This comparative study, now nearing completion, has set a number of problems of comparison, not only between one geographical locality and another, but also between the religious practice of one period of time and that of another, between the practice of one denomination and that of another.

History is necessary to the sociologist of religion for a correct understanding of contemporary religious matters. Almost all churches and denominations claim some kind of historical continuity, which in turn has a visible effect on their interpretation of the contemporary scene, on their teaching role as it affects their followers and on their own structures. The Roman Catholic Church, the most spectacular example, the Church of England and all the leading Nonconformist denominations are bound to a greater or lesser extent by their traditions. The development of traditional practice in religious institutions takes place often over long periods of time, and therefore to understand a contemporary practice usually requires a knowledge of the reasons for its development in history.

The pioneer of historical research in the sociological study of religious practice has been Gabriel LeBras,[2] who has demonstrated clearly, within the framework of the Roman Catholic Church in France, how complex and multivarious any religious practice usually is. His work and influence must be considered one of the most important contributions to the sociological study of Christian practice both in historical and contemporary settings. Many of the categories he employs are applicable, to a greater or lesser extent, to practice within the different denominations of a pluralist society like Great Britain.

Bristol and Marseilles: the problems

The questions the author was concerned to answer at the outset of his research went rather as follows: Was there a decline in the influence of religion over men's minds in cities during the nineteenth century? If this was so, was this decline limited to cities or did it extend into the countryside also? If such a decline of religious influence did take place, then what were its characteristics? Did institutional religion suffer? Was it rather the influence of the giant new industrial cities, of certain of their pressures, which exercised an adverse effect on the practice of religion? Was this an international situation?

As the work progressed however it became clear, that behind these superficial problems lay another set of wider and more fundamental ones. If such a decline did take place under the pressure of industrialization, what is it to be compared with historically? Could it not be claimed that it was not really a decline, but rather a reorientation? Had there not been a re-alignment of 'religious' society along altered values, to correspond with a global society which had become much more complicated and much more specialized? Conversely would it not be fair to say that many men who 'practised' their religion in earlier times, did so because if they did not, society would punish them severely, by burning them at the stake, by imposing heavy fines and so on? It seems clear that the myth of the Middle Ages as the 'age of faith', held dear by many, is partly a false conception.

Theoretical lines of approach

Mid-nineteenth-century cities provide examples of 'secularized' societies, as this term is understood by Howard Becker in his sacred-secular continuum.[3] As industrialization created these cities, thus providing a basis for their enlargement, country people left their villages and their traditional, more sacred, way of life, to become immersed in these turbulent secular communities. In doing so these country people lost many of the traditional motivations to religious practice, which had made such good sense in the village. One follows here the theory of the French Jesuit sociologist, Emile Pin,[4] who has distinguished three primary and three secondary motivations for religious practice. Thus, for example, one primary motivation is the 'cosmological' motivation or need to reconcile oneself, through religious practice, with a mysterious and uncontrollable natural element. Clearly this must have been strong in traditional rural communities, but must have been almost non-existent in the urban communities of 1850. One of the secondary motivations is the 'spontaneous cultural' motivation prevalent in small, rural, pre-industrial communities, where communal custom imposes religious observance of ceremonies. Faithfulness to custom itself is important and expresses the continuity of the group. Clearly the country migrants of early industrialization found in the secular city that all was constantly changing, that continuity as expressed through custom played no part, by definition, in those new communities. Thus this motivation was removed for those country migrants newly arrived in the cities. However the development of commercial and industrial cities, from the medieval period onwards, and the stimulating intellectual atmosphere often to be found in them also encouraged certain forms of religious reform and renewal, often at variance with the traditional Christian institutions.

Thus in the field of religious practice the nineteenth-century industrial cities of France and England presented two important factors: on the one hand the newly arrived migrants found some of their motivations to practise swept away, and consequently many of this group ceased to practise in any other way than sometimes observing the rites of passage; on the other hand the special atmosphere of these cities led to new religious movements.

1. *Overall religious attendance*

As a superficial indicator of the influence of religion in Bristol, a study has been made of the rates of Sunday attendance at places of worship between 1841 and 1881.

Three surveys of attendance at Sunday worship were carried out during the period: one in 1841, organized and administered by the Bristol Statistical Society;[5] one in 1851 organized and administered on a national basis by the Government;[6] and the third in 1881, carried out under the auspices of the *Western Daily Press*.[7] The statistics presented by all three require very careful treatment, as the methods employed provide opportunities for considerable, if varying, degrees of error. However, if attendance figures from these three surveys are divided into those concerning the ancient city and those concerning the suburban areas, it becomes clear that the real challenge to the churches, as far as accommodation and pastoral effort were concerned, came in the suburban areas. In 1841 it is clear too that the churches were almost all poorly equipped to meet the greatly increased population of the suburbs. Thus, according to the 1841 survey, while city attendance stood at an index of 37,[8] that of the suburbs only reached 18. The 1851 Ecclesiastical Census gives comparable respective figures of 72 and 42. By 1881, with all the denominations fully aware of the enormous and rapidly growing suburban populations, the indices were respectively 59 and 43.

By further sub-division one can arrive at interesting differences between various types of suburb. Thus the fashionable suburb of Clifton, whose population increased from 14,177 in 1841 to 26,364 in 1881, had indices of 43 in 1841, 69 in 1851 and 82 in 1881. Undoubtedly this area was very well provided with places of worship, many new buildings being erected there during the period. On the other hand the Out Parish of St Philip and St Jacob, the residence of a large part of the poorest labouring classes, presents an entirely different aspect. The population increased from 21,590 in 1841 to 50,108 in 1881. Indices of attendance stood at 14 in 1841, at 40 in 1851 and at 24 in 1881.

In the socio-economically similar suburb of Bedminster the overall picture is remarkably similar. The population increased from 17,862 in 1841 to 44,759 in 1881. Indices of attendance stood at 13 in 1841, at 20 in 1851 and at 26 in 1881.

2. *The Church of England*

If one examines these surveys of attendance for each denomination, it becomes clear that the Church of England made a very considerable effort during the period to improve its position. In 1831 there were 24 places of worship belonging to the Established Church. By 1881 there were 58. Indices of attendance were as follows:

	Ancient city	Suburbs	All
1841	17	7	12
1851	26	21	23
1881	19	20	20

The disparity between ancient city and suburbs, so clear in 1841, had been almost completely removed by 1881, even though the size of the population of the suburbs increased dramatically during the period. However this enormous pastoral effort may be interpreted only as a holding operation. There was not really any progress made towards the evangelization of the large proportion of the population who appear, from the figures of these surveys, not to have attended places of worship.

3. *Other denominations*

Attendance figures for the leading Nonconformist denominations have been analysed in the same way. Important points to come from these analyses are that attendances at Independent or Congregationalist places of worship appear to have fallen by the end of the period; for all kinds of Methodists, indices of attendance are higher in 1881 than in 1841, but rather lower than in 1851. The Baptists appear to have maintained their position. All three denominations lost worshippers in the ancient city area, where they were best equipped: this loss must be attributed largely to the migration of city residents to the suburbs, where they transferred their worshipping allegiance to suburban chapels. The Roman Catholics increased their number considerably, through immigration, but their attendance figures do not appear to reflect fully the natural growth to be expected from such an influx of immigrants. The Quakers, typically, remained a very small but highly influential body.

4. *Bristol and elsewhere*

It is perhaps interesting, at this point, to compare the situation in Bristol in 1851 with that of other large cities in the country. In the eight towns of 100,000 inhabitants or more, but excluding London, the Anglican index of attendance was 17; in Bristol, as already noted, it was 23; in London it was 21. For non-Anglican attendance, the overall figure was 24; in Bristol it was 31; in London it was 17. Thus the total attendance indices were 41 in the eight large towns, which includes Bristol of course, in Bristol 54 and in London 38.[9] Clearly Bristol had a much higher than average attendance index and yet, even there, the churches failed to provide adequately for the growing population.

5. *A labouring class suburb*

A much more detailed study has been made of a poor, labouring class suburb, situated (in 1831) on the edge of the city, in order to examine in detail the various aspects of religious practice and action in such a milieu. Part of the Out Parish of St Philip and St Jacob was selected as a suitable area – this included the parishes of Holy Trinity and St Jude. This latter parish consisted entirely of a slum area, among the most impoverished in Bristol in the nineteenth century.

Living conditions were, as might be expected, very poor. By contemporary standards, housing was entirely inadequate. By the 1880's certain improvements were to be observed in the quarter. There had been a definite drop in the crime rate, for example, but housing conditions remained very poor.

All the denominations already mentioned were represented in the area, but, as stated above, levels of attendance at worship were considerably lower than in the middle class suburb of Clifton.

In 1841, in the area of the two parishes which had a total population of 10,655, there were available some 2,435 seats in all places of worship, while the average attendance would appear to have been of the order of 1,230. That is to say that about half the seats available were occupied on an average Sunday. Therefore it can be claimed that the position of religion among the labouring classes involved much more than a lack of places of worship and seating. There was clearly, in 1841, a considerable degree of abstention from Sunday worship. By 1881 the two parishes had a total population of some 19,250. There were 5,092 seats available in all places of worship and 6,444 attendances, which represents quite a considerable increase. However, by comparison with figures for 1851, there appears to have been a slight relative decline, although absolute figures for attendances and population both increase. From this and other evidence the conclusion may be drawn that increases in attendances at Anglican churches did not keep pace with population increase. Nonconformist attendances, more difficult to interpret, fluctuated during the period. The Methodist schism of mid-century, for example, led to the establishment of another possible place of worship in the area for the Methodist worshipper. Many attended Methodist and Independent places of worship, who were not technically members of these denominations.

Analysis of the rite of baptism for the locality shows that the number of newly-born children baptized into the Church of England was well below the national average. The numbers baptized into other denominations were very small during the period. It may even be claimed that many infants were not baptized at all, and therefore most probably not registered. From examination of Methodist baptismal (and marriage) registers, it may well be assumed that many Methodists preferred to baptize their children (and to wed) in the Established Church, while remaining at the same time practising members of the local chapel.[10]

A study of the sacrament of communion has also been made for the labouring class quarter. In considering this sacrament one must constantly bear in mind that it played different roles for different denominations at different periods of time. When Bishop C. J. Ellicott took over the Diocese of Gloucester and Bristol in 1864, he was dissatisfied with the situation he found in this respect.[11] Indeed the 1841 survey spells it out only too clearly.[12] Thus in the City of Bristol the figures for communicants represent only about 15% of average Anglican attendances, while for the Independents, Wesleyans and Baptists, the figures were respectively 27%, 27%, and 49%.

In the years following 1864, Bishop Ellicott campaigned in his diocese for more frequent celebration of Holy Communion, and consequently, he felt, increased numbers of communicants. This

E

policy met with a considerable measure of success throughout the diocese, though not in Holy Trinity parish where in three summer months in 1880 there was an average of 58 communicants on a Sunday out of an average attendance of at least 1,500 and much more probably 2,300.[13] Clearly the sacrament played a negligible part in the normal life of the parish. For St Jude's parish in the heart of the slum there was an average of about 10 communicants on an ordinary Sunday in 1881, when an average Sunday attendance was probably about 260.[14] If one considers that St Jude's had adopted an Anglo-Catholic liturgy and could therefore be expected to stress the sacramental life as important, one acquires a much more realistic picture of the considerable measure of indifference then prevailing in the parish. The local Roman Catholic church of St Nicholas presents a rather different situation. In 1858 for example, it was calculated that some 33% of the parish made an Easter Communion, while in 1894 this proportion had risen to 42%.[15] In one Methodist chapel in Bristol in 1880 88 communicants were noticed at an evening service out of a congregation of about 410, which indicates a proportion of about one-fifth.[16]

MARSEILLES: 1830–1880

1. *Overall religious attendance*

One important reason why Marseilles was chosen for comparison with Bristol is that the size of the population and of population increase in both cities were very similar during the nineteenth century. Only in the twentieth century did Marseilles forge ahead to to become a more heavily populated city. Thus the built-up area of Marseilles contained 82,585 people in 1808, while that of Bristol had 85,921 in 1811. Similarly in 1886 Marseilles had 289,433 inhabitants, while Bristol had 291,740 in 1891.

The only sources of information relating to attendance at religious worship are the enquiries carried out by the Bishop of Marseilles, and relating naturally to the Roman Catholic Church. Indeed only one such survey was carried out during the period of time under consideration, in the years 1862/63.[17] However the Abbé F. L. Charpin, in his interesting work on the sacrament of baptism in Marseilles in the nineteenth and twentieth centuries,[18] concludes that the relationship between religious worship on Sundays and the length of delay between birth and baptism is a constant one. Thus, armed with the correlation to be calculated from the 1862/63 survey and his own research on the delay before baptism for that year, he is able, convincingly to establish by calculation from baptismal statistics, indices for Sunday worship for years when episcopal surveys were not carried out. Thus in 1825 the proportion of the population who attended Sunday worship regularly was 51%; in 1841 it was 47%, in 1862 it stood at 38%, and by 1901 it had dropped to 16%. Thus Charpin concludes that the absolute number of those attending Sunday worship in Marseilles increased up to about 1861, doubtless as a consequence of the general increase of the city's population, but that after this date the figure has remained approximately stationary despite the very considerable increases in total population. Thus in terms of church attendance and of parish endeavour, churches have been filled, since the mid-nineteenth century with the same numbers of faithful, who have represented an increasingly reduced proportion of the total population.[19]

During the period studied the number of non-Catholics among the population of Marseilles increased sharply. Thus, while those describing themselves as Catholics increased from 190,716 in 1851 to 296,101 in 1872,[20] Calvinist Protestants rose from 3,082 to 9,670, and Lutherans from 170 to 2,972. The Jewish population rose from 986 to 2,662, and those of other faiths, including the Orthodox, from 184 to 1,270. Thus during the twenty-five years following 1850, there was a considerable increase in the non-Catholic population. Charpin attributes this, where Protestants are concerned, to immigration from Protestant areas of France.[21]

As with Bristol, it is clear that levels of Sunday attendance in Marseilles varied from area to area. Thus the information provided by the 1862/63 diocesan survey can be analysed to show that the parishes of the central city, of mixed middle and working class composition, probably had a level of Sunday attendance of around 35% – perhaps rather more – while the parishes of the suburbs, almost exclusively working class, and involving some 77,000 inhabitants in a total population of 228,714, had a level of only 26%. The rural areas of the Commune of Marseilles, predictably, showed much higher levels of attendance, varying from 62% to 43%. Again one should question the reliability of these statistics.[22]

It is clear that the Roman Catholic Church made serious efforts to provide adequate spiritual facilities for the immensely increased population. In 1821 the number of parishes in the built-up area was 12, in 1886 it had risen to 30. The average size of the parish was 7,380 persons in 1821 and 9,650 in 1886, while the number of active clergy in the parishes increased from 51 in 1821 to 117 in 1886. In evaluating such figures, one must always bear in mind that a large number of religious orders had chapels open to the public for Sunday worship, that the men's orders consisted to a great extent of religious who were ordained priests, and who were often engaged in pastoral endeavour, which was supplementary to the work of the parishes. In this non-parish context, which one is tempted, from the purely sociological aspect, to liken to the role of the Nonconformist chapels in Bristol, statistics are even rarer than for the diocesan parishes. In 1862, there were, it was claimed by the *curé* of the parish in which the Jesuit church stood, some 4,000 people who attended Sunday worship in that church, and who worshipped therefore in a certain sense outside the diocesan authority.

2. *A labouring-class suburb*

As for Bristol, a special study has been made of a poor labouring-class inner suburb of Marseilles, in order to examine in greater detail the different aspects of religious practice and action in such an area. A district in the northern suburbs of the city was selected as suitable. This included three parishes: St Lazare, St Mauront and St Charles-extra muros often referred to as the Belle-de-Mai. This district, immediately to the north of the main railway station of St Charles, contained two of the largest sugar refineries and a large tobacco factory, besides a number of military barracks.

From the 1840's onwards there took place a fairly considerable amount of emigration from the old city to this new and cheaper district. Industry developed in this area, thus creating jobs and adding the further attraction of work. With this development there sprang into being whole new housing areas in the parishes of St Mauront and the Belle-de-Mai. In 1860 the Belle-de-Mai had about 5,000 inhabitants; by 1865 this had almost doubled to about 10,000; and by 1875 the population of this one parish had reached 15 or 16,000 inhabitants.[23]

About 1870, 25% of the population of this area consisted of people who had come out from the centre of the city; 25% consisted of people who had come into Marseilles from the immediately surrounding countryside and neighbouring *départements*. The remaining half of the population were immigrants from further afield, notably from Italy, particularly from Piedmont and Tuscany. Between 1860 and 1875 Italian immigration into this district was considerable. Though they found French difficult to learn, they mastered Provençal relatively easily. In fact Provençal remained the most readily understood language in this area at this time, although its usage was disappearing in the central city. The Italians were almost all of peasant origin and mostly became unskilled labourers, doing the heavy jobs in the factories of the quarter. Poor workshop conditions were made worse by the failure on the part of many factories to observe Sunday as a day of rest, and the very long working hours.[24]

People changed their lodgings often; common law marriages were frequent; the care of children was very deficient, especially where both parents worked. No crèche existed in the area before 1875. Cafés, bars and drinking houses were legion and there were a number of very low-class brothels.

In these conditions levels of attendance at Sunday worship were almost certainly low. Reliable statistics do not exist. In 1861 and 1863 the *curé* of the Belle-de-Mai claimed that two-thirds of the population worshipped on a Sunday. In 1861, according to him, the population stood at 7,000 and in 1863 at about 10,000. However, his estimate appears ill-founded. In the neighbouring parish of St Mauront, with a population of the same socio-economic character, the *curé* made much more modest claims for his parish, suggesting attendance levels of 23% for 1861 and 20% for 1863. These levels are much more realistic and those for the Belle-de-Mai were probably very similar.[25]

Where Easter communion was concerned, figures are likely to be somewhat more accurate. For the Belle-de-Mai in 1861, 2,190 communions were claimed, 31% of the population. In 1863 only 1,700 communions at Easter were claimed on an increased population, resulting in a percentage of 17%. In 1871 there were 2,000 Easter communions on a greatly increased population.[26] In the parish of St Mauront the proportions of the total population receiving Easter communion were 21% in 1861, 20% in 1863 and an estimated 11% in 1872.

Clearly, as the period proceeds, the numbers attending Sunday worship represent an increasingly small proportion of the total population.

CONCLUSION

In summing up some of these results, one may be permitted here to stress that in an article of this length, only very little of the information obtained can be discussed. A full analysis of it has yet to be made, and therefore any conclusions presented here can only be regarded as tentative.

Was there a decline in the influence of religion over men's minds in cities in the nineteenth century? This was certainly the case in both Bristol and Marseilles, though in both cities this was greater for members of the labouring classes than for those of the middle or upper artisan classes. By the 1830's in Bristol and by the 1850's in Marseilles there was already massive abstention from worship among the labouring classes, and it is felt that the process of immigration from rural to urban society, with its accompanying mutation of motivations to worship, was largely responsible for this abstention.[27] A rather special type of evangelical apostolate was required in towns, where the immigrants were concerned. In England the early Methodists were partially successful in this work, while in Marseilles attempts in this direction were made by the Jesuits of the Mission de France church and by the Abbé Timon-David.

At first glance it would appear that the pluralist society of Bristol was better equipped in clergy and in places of worship of all denominations than was the largely Roman Catholic organization of Marseilles. Thus one can abstract the following tables:[28]

BRISTOL				MARSEILLES	
	Anglican churches	Dissenting chapels etc.	Total		RC parishes
1831	24	36	60	1821	12
1881	58	106	164	1886	30

BRISTOL				MARSEILLES	
	Anglican clergy	Dissenting ministers etc.	Total		RC parish clergy	Total of active priests
1831	35	26	61	1821	51	134
1881	107	69	176	1886	117	315

Analysis of such tables is made rather difficult because, as already mentioned, there were in Marseilles a host of small chapels, and sometimes large churches, belonging to religious orders, all of which fell outside the parochial system, just as, in Bristol, the dissenting chapels fell outside the parochial system of the Established Church. However in Marseilles each of these chapels of the male religious orders might well have attached to it half-a-dozen or more religious who were also ordained priests. In Bristol, the Dissenting chapels, particularly those of the Methodists, had fewer ministers than places of worship. Thus in 1881 in Bristol there were 106 dissenting places of worship in the charge of 69 clergy.[29] Therefore, though a case might possibly be made out for relatively more places of worship in Bristol than in Marseilles, it is quite clear that the number of specialized, full-time personnel was greater in Marseilles than in Bristol.

Whatever the organizational differences between the two cities, the inability to cope with the immigrants from rural societies and with their rather special spiritual needs, appears to have been common to both cities, despite the very considerable differences of religious tradition and practice. This inability had its more obvious practical expression in the relative shortage of places of worship and clergy for those areas of the cities being rapidly expanded by immigration. But perhaps more fundamental than this were the images presented by the different religious institutions and the nature and quality of their pastoral action.

NOTES

1. David A. Martin, *A Sociology of English Religion*, London: SCM Press and Heinemann, 1967, p. 122.

2. Gabriel LeBras, *Etudes de Sociologie religieuse*, Paris: Presses universitaires de France, 2 vols., 1956. This work includes articles demonstrating his main lines of approach.

3. Howard Becker, 'Current sacred-secular theory and its development', in: Howard Becker and Alvin Boskoff (eds.), *Modern Sociological Theory*, New York: Dryden Press, 1957, pp. 133–185.

4. Emile Pin, 'Les motivations des conduites religieuses et le passage d'une civilisation pré-technique à une civilisation technique', *Social Compass* 13.1, 1966, pp. 25–37.

5. Bristol Statistical Society: *5th Annual Report* 1841, Bristol Reference Library.

6. Ecclesiastical Census, 1851. *Census Returns*, H.O. 129.330/4. Public Record Office.

7. *Western Daily Press: Religious Census*, 2 Nov 1881. Bristol Reference Library.

8. The index of attendance used throughout this article refers to the total number of attendances expressed as a percentage of the total population figure for the area under consideration. A proportion of people attended places of worship more than once on a Sunday. On the other hand many young children could not be expected to attend at all.

See also K. S. Inglis, 'Patterns of Worship in 1851', *Journal of Ecclesiastical History* 11, 1960, pp. 74–86.

9. For the basic figures from which these indices were calculated, I am indebted to Professor Harold Perkin, University of Lancaster.

10. St Jude's parish: *Baptismal Registers*, 1846–1883, Holy Trinity parish: *Baptismal Registers*, 1832–1883, Old Market Street Methodist: *Baptismal Registers*, 1838–1884, Stapleton Road Independent: *Baptismal Register*, 1868–71, St Nicholas R.C. parish: *Baptismal registers*, 1856–1880.

11. C. J. Ellicott, D.D., *A Charge to the Clergy of the Diocese*, 1864. Bristol Reference Library.

12. Bristol Statistical Society: op. cit.

13. Holy Trinity parish: Preacher's book, 1880–1888.

14. St Jude's parish: Preacher's book, 1876–1884.

15. Roman Catholic Diocese of Clifton: *Visitation Returns for 1858/9 and 1895*. Clifton Diocesan Archives.

16. R. D. Robjent, *The Bristol Nonconformist Sunday Services*. About 1880/1881. Bristol Reference Library.

17. *Pastoral Enquiry 1862/63*. Archives of the Archidiocese of Marseilles. Dossier 236, 2 and 3.

18. F. L. Charpin, *Pratique religieuse et formation d'une grande ville: Marseille 1806–1956*, Paris 1964.

19. F. L. Charpin, *op. cit.*, pp. 152 ff.

20. These figures relate to the population of the Commune of Marseilles, including large rural districts as well as the built-up area.

21. F. L. Charpin, *op. cit.*, pp. 206 ff.

22. *Ibid.*

23. Jean Chélini, *Genèse et évolution d'une paroisse suburbaine marseillaise-Le Bon Pasteur*, Marseille: Imprimerie Saint-Léon, 1953, ch. 1, pp. 1–26.

24. *Ibid.*

25. *Pastoral Enquiry, 1862/63*. Archives of the Archidiocese of Marseilles. Dossier 236, 2 and 3.

26. *Pastoral Enquiry 1870/72*, Archives of the Archidiocese of Marseilles. Dossier 236, 4.

27. The situation of the countryside surrounding Bristol in 1851 has been analysed by the present writer: R. M. Goodridge, 'The Religious Condition of the West Country in 1851', *Social Compass* 14.4, 1967, pp. 285–96.

28. Figures for Bristol are abstracted from *Mathew's Bristol Directory 1831–1881*. Those for Marseilles are quoted by F. L. Charpin, *op. cit.*, p. 204.

29. Figures from *Mathew's Bristol Directory 1881*. These figures also include Roman Catholic churches and priests.

8 Muslims in Britain

Eric Butterworth

AMONG the non-Christian migrants to Britain the largest group is of Muslims. The majority have arrived within the space of the last ten years, and only a few were in residence before the beginning of the Second World War. These exceptions usually settled in seaports such as London, Cardiff, Liverpool, and South Shields. Their lives, over the period of time since about 1919, when many of the settlements were founded, showed a continuing group cohesion but also forms of adaptation to the wider society. In part this arose because of the intermarriage that took place but also because of the relatively small scale of settlement.

The new situation that is developing contrasts with the old in a number of ways. In the first place it is more dynamic. The number of Muslims is increasing rapidly, and many more children are now being born in Britain of Muslim parents. It is also a settlement which takes place in some of the largest cities and towns. Virtually all Muslims in Britain, coming though they do from rural backgrounds, live near the centres of urban areas. As time passes, however, there is an unmistakable tendency for dispersion to take place within certain groups, and the idea of the monolithic community resisting all kinds of encroachments from the outside has to be qualified in various ways. The extent to which a 'community response' arises is, and will continue to be, in part determined by the attitudes of the host community and the kinds of situations in which contact is made, to which both migrants and hosts bring numerous preconceptions. A further important qualification which is necessary relates to the lower incidence of intermarriage than in the earliest settlements. In general the settlement consists, where families are present, of parents both of whom have been born in the Indian sub-continent.

The great majority of Muslims in Britain today are from the Indian sub-continent. Almost certainly there are at least 200,000 of them, and if children born here are included then the figure will be around a quarter of a million. Moreover, some thousands of children are born in Britain to Muslim parents each year. Numbers are expected to continue to rise. There could be a community of three-quarters of a million by the year 2000 at present rates of increase.

Within the religious group many ethnic groups are represented. From Pakistan there are Kashmiris, Punjabis and Bengalis, and from India Gujeratis. In many respects there are great differences between the groups from these regions. Bengalis live over a thousand miles apart from the Punjabis of West Pakistan, and ways of life may be very different. A small number of other Muslim migrants, usually first or second generation settlers in East Africa, share many aspects of the culture of West Pakistanis, though there are differences which derive from their more urban and cosmopolitan background.

Other Muslims in Britain include Arabs and Somalis from East Africa, Hausas from Nigeria, Turkish Cypriots, and some Muslims from south-east Asia, but the focus of this article will be upon those who have settled in Britain recently from the Indian sub-continent, together with an occasional note about those from East Africa whose experience will be similar in some respects.

The distinctions which exist between different sects in the Muslim world must have some consequences for the conduct of the individual. The majority of Muslims in Britain are Sunnis, from Pakistan, but there are also Shias from the same areas, and other groups, usually from a distinct locale, such as the Amadiyas from Lahore and Qadian, Ismailies from East Africa, and Ethna-Asharies from the Middle East as well as parts of Pakistan. The extent to which their beliefs as members of the sects, and their ways of life on coming to Britain are distinct must affect their adaptation.

The basic questions to be asked are about the effects of life in Britain on the religious observance, beliefs, and ways of life of Muslims. The amount of attention which has been given to the subject is limited, in part because of the short time the majority have been in this country. But they are none the less important questions because they pose problems of identity and adaptation for an increasing number in the future.

The first issue is the kind of beliefs about religion and their religious and cultural practices the Muslims bring with them, and the rights and obligations that they share. Then there are the situations into which they move here, as compared with those in their country of origin. Broadly speaking, the main distinctions that arise, and they are much more clear cut for Muslims than for the other religious groups, are between the stages of all-male settlement and those when families are brought over. The relationship between the kind of settlement, its population, the extent to which there is a high concentration of Muslims in the area, its social structure, its patterns of leadership, both political and religious, and its contacts with the individuals and the institutions, including the Christian churches, of the host society need to be looked at. Contrary to the rather simple image which many have of these processes, they are often extremely complex. Whilst it is true that there is a 'British' climate of race relations, as defined in a general sense, there is also great diversity, and the situations are not rigid and defined in a way more typical of, for example, parts of the United States. Finally, questions are raised, and some evidence examined, about the prospects for the future, and in particular about the changes that could take place.

The beliefs of the Muslim centre around the meaning of Islam, which is peace. There are three areas in which this applies: within the individual, with others, and with God. Islam teaches human beings in all parts of the world, irrespective of race and country, to worship one God. Humanity is one family, and distinctions on the grounds of race, colour, wealth or descent do not matter.[1] (At the same time, the social structure of Muslim countries tends to show great concentrations of wealth and power.)

A Muslim, a follower of Islam, is taught that there is one true God, and that Mohammed (Peace be upon him) is the last prophet to come on earth. This is the first of the so-called Pillars of Islam. He believes in the Angels, the Holy Revealed Books, the Divinely Inspired Messengers of God who include Adam, Abraham, Moses and Jesus (as well as Mohammed), the Day of Judgment, and the premeasurement of good and evil.

'The institution of Muslim prayer rests upon the precept of the Qur'an and the example of the Prophet.'[2] Tradition has laid down that the call to prayer, Salat, should be heeded five times a day at specific times. There is a strict ordering of the prayers, which may otherwise be invalid, and of the ritual that goes with them. Once a week, on a Friday, the faithful should take part in a special ceremony, the Friday prayer. During this time economic life should be suspended.

Other institutions include the fast, which is mainly connected with abstinence for one lunar month during Ramadan. (It was not foreseen that this would move throughout the course of the year, as did the Muslim calendar which is based on twelve lunar months.) The believer is required to abstain entirely from food, drink, tobacco, sexual relations, and some other things, between sunrise and sunset. The physical and mental effects of the fast of Ramadan are considerable, and it is only obligatory on adults in full possession of their physical and mental faculties. At the same time many children and young people appear to be encouraged to fulfil the fast.

The pilgrimage to Mecca, the *hajj*, should be accomplished at least once in a lifetime if the resources are available. It may be undertaken by proxy if necessary.

The remaining pillar of Islam, the payment of *zikat*, or legal alms, is graduated according to certain principles laid down by the Prophet. There are different rates according to the source of income, ranging from twenty per cent on minerals and treasure trove to proportions around two per cent for cattle reared on pastures. *Zikat* is assessable only on persons who have at the end of the year more in value than the prescribed minimum.[3] The level for the majority is at the rate of about two and a half per cent of the value of income.

The culture and traditions of Islam have numerous social consequences which can best be considered in relation to settlement in Britain. The structure of beliefs outlined provides a complete way of life for Muslims coming to this country, coming as they do from rural areas which are often remote. The link between beliefs and practices tends to be closer than is usually the case with the observance of Christianity in the advanced societies of the West. Islam is linked in most parts of the world to an organization of society securely based on a familial and kinship model. The idea of original sin has no place in belief.[4] Children are born without sin, and sin is an acquisition and not a heritage. The mediation between man and God which is performed by the priesthood in, for example, the Roman Catholic church has no parallel. The life of the Muslim is one, whether carried on in the mosque, the market-place, the factory or the school.

The relationship between beliefs and conduct is best understood when we observe how life and belief are linked in an all-embracing way. The social functions of religion include that of symbolic integration, which was crucial to the definition used by Durkheim. Society is an organization of groups and interests that often conflict, and for Durkheim the solidarity that arose within society came mainly from the religious bonds which transcend sectional interests.

The Punjabi, the Kashmiri and the Bengali come, it would appear, from rural environments where this integration on the basis of religion takes place, and where few of the influences of the town, and the diversification of belief and conduct which follow, are to be found.

Social control in that setting is exercised in a mainly informal way, being concerned to ensure that conduct is in accordance with the norms of the society from which they have come. There are two kinds of social control which may be distinguished; that from outside and that from within. That from outside, in the country of Pakistan, is the political power of the Muslim state of Pakistan. (For the Indian Muslims the position is different.) The legitimating function of religion is present whenever obedience to the agencies of social control is interpreted as religious duty. The most powerful social controls relate to the structure of marriage and property, and for the Muslim these are protected with a particular intensity.

The social control that comes from within is usually called 'conscience' in Christian society. The need for an internalization of the norms to ensure conformity is particularly important. Where the structure of social control is relatively all-embracing and permanent, in the village, the extent to which internalization takes place may be less than in situations where there is greater permissiveness and choice. In an urban society which is advanced, as in Britain, the internalization of the norms may not stand up against the new attractions to behave in different kinds of ways. The factors involved are the opportunities to behave differently, the operation of the social controls in the immediate setting of the household (in fact, the way in which deviant behaviour is regarded), the extent to which a kind of 'conscience' operates, and the structure of leadership and its preoccupation with religion as a force which insulates and reassures the group against outside influences which are seen to be inferior and threatening.

Obvious problems arise for the Muslim in the matter of religious observance. It is extremely difficult to find time during the normal working day for the two of the five daily prayers which should be said. This is particularly the case in a relatively crowded works because of the need not to be interrupted during the rituals and the importance of the particular area used by the person praying not being crossed by others.

At Ramadan, which in 1968, began during November, most Muslims in Britain fast. It is 'a common participation in an act of self-discipline'.[5] This raises numerous questions about their spiritual and physical needs during this time. A few employers are prepared to make special provision for Muslims to have a private room set aside for prayer at this time, but this is usually a time of year when misunderstandings between employers and employees over the necessity of prayer during the day can result in summary dismissals and a worsening of industrial relations. Too many employers have been less than accommodating in this situation. For example, it was recently reported in *The Guardian* that only two employers in the whole of Sheffield were making special arrangements for Muslim employees during Ramadan.[6] This is the main time of year when the reaffirmation of religious values and commitment takes place.

Mosques attract relatively small numbers of Muslims in Britain with the exception of one or two large ones in centres such as Birmingham. In one town with a small settlement of about 1,500 it was estimated that only a dozen or so went there regularly to pray. The mosque was a converted house and this in itself limits its use. At the time of the Eid festivals, at the end of Ramadan, a local hall was hired and usually attracted 800 people each year.

Increasingly mosques are used by schoolchildren. In the case mentioned above a full-time priest was appointed in 1966 and he looks after the children who, by arrangement with the local education authority, come for prayers every Friday afternoon. In many Muslim homes one finds collecting boxes for the mosque – in some cases this is for the mosque which it is hoped to build. For many years now Muslims in Bradford have had plans ready to build a large mosque on the model of the main one in Karachi, but no start has been made yet. In another town in East Lancashire where the Muslim population is over 3,000, and where there are virtually no other ethnic groups, about sixty people regularly attend the mosque. This is a converted Sunday School, and there are satisfactory arrangements for ablutions which are particularly important since before prayer the worshipper must submit to special conditions of personal and external purity, which require him to be washed with water which is legally pure. The worshipper must 'be free of every defilement (*hadath*), great or small'.[7]

As the communities are established mosques will be provided with satisfactory accommodation. The few attenders in the examples given do not necessarily imply a turning away from religious observance. There are no formal services which are comparable with those in Christian Churches. The believer is part of the group by his prayers and also by the prohibitions prescribed by his religion or the traditions which have developed along with it.

Moreover, as one informant writes:

> There are many Islamic Missionary Societies whose main aim is to propagate Islam amongst the Muslims in Britain, and persuade them to go to the mosque for prayers. They travel from one town to another on their own initiative and in a voluntary capacity. They would stay for the night in one of the rooms of the mosque by sleeping on cushions etc. which they bring themselves and then move on to an other town. Besides the Missionary Societies there are many eminent Muslim priests from Pakistan and India who would travel to many different cities and deliver sermons in different mosques or halls, which are hired for that particular purpose.

This point about the establishment of religious associations is also made by Desai when he says:

> Muslims and Sikhs have established religious associations wherever they have settled in the United Kingdom as communities and as soon as these communities have been able to bear the cost. The Muslims have mosques organized on a linguistic-regional basis (although there is no religious injunction behind such a limitation) . . .[8]

The payment of *zikat* is undertaken rarely in Britain. This arises in part because of the high level of taxation, but many appear to fulfil the payment by means of financial contributions made through their families in their countries of origin. The only commitments that the faithful Muslim has in this country is to support the mosque. It was the opinion of some Muslims who were consulted that *zikat* was not levied where the society had large numbers of non-Muslims. In some areas an alternative tax, *jazia*, is levied on people for their own protection.

The religious leadership is bound up with the general question of leadership in the community and will be dealt with later. At this time it is necessary to look at the characteristics of the settlement of Muslims in Britain. The peak of the migration of men was from the late 1950's up to 1962. Since 1964 far more women and children have been entering the country. The change in the pattern of entry is partly a consequence of the Commonwealth Immigrants Act of 1962 and the White Paper of 1965 which restricted the numbers of workers allowed in, and partly in consequence of growing accumulation of capital which allows Muslims to pay for their families to join them and allows them to afford accommodation for them. At the census of 1961, among Pakistanis, the ratio of men to women was of the order of twelve to one.[9] The proportion of children up to school leaving age, the lowest of all the migrant groups in 1961, is now increasing rapidly because of entry from the countries of origin and also the birth rate in Britain.

The stages so far have included the first, when the distinctive features arose from the overwhelming predominance of men, and the second, when an increasing proportion of the men who settled here have been bringing over families to join them. The average amount of time between the arrival of the man and his family, in those cases when the man brings his family over, appears to be between five and seven years, but there may be great variations. Despite the virtual ban on the entry of workers there are still tens of thousands of men who will bring families over within the next few years. A relatively small proportion only are professional men, the majority of these being doctors. They are less likely to be married, for one thing, but if they are married they are likely to bring their families over earlier than is the case with married men engaged in manual work. The worker, in mill, factory, foundry or whatever, may take much longer to save the required amount of money for the air fares (in most cases) and for the indispensable minimum of accommodation after arrival. The variables here include the availability of well-paid work and the amount of overtime. In some parts of the country relatively low wage rates can go along with high rates of earnings, and a high level of saving, because of overtime and work at the weekends: the woollen industry of West Yorkshire is a good example of this, with night shifts, for which there is more pay, being staffed by Pakistanis and Indians, who can also obtain large amounts of overtime. Working weeks of sixty hours and more are not uncommon, with obvious consequences for the social life of the men. The costs of housing and accommodation are also relevant: they are, for example, much higher in the Greater London area and the West Midlands than in some other parts of the country. Houses can still be bought in West Yorkshire for £700 or so, providing accommodation of several bedrooms in addition to living rooms.

The relatively long-term all-male situation means that a much greater part of the life of the individual will be spent within the confines of the group. Even at work Muslims may be members of groups from the same areas: the classic situation where this applies is in the woollen industry, where, as just mentioned, many night shifts of mills are staffed almost entirely by them.

Institutions for leisure-time activities are usually within the area in which the men live. The concentration of Muslim settlement gives cohesion to the life of the individual in every sphere. Despite the existence of discrimination the group is relatively insulated and protected. The term accommodation is used to describe the minimal adaptation and acceptance that takes place in this situation in these main areas of life. Whereas West Indians desire to assimilate to British ways, Muslims wish to preserve their religious and cultural identity. Their aim is rather cultural pluralism, whereby they can remain separate for certain purposes but also be accepted as equals. The definition of integration given by Mr Roy Jenkins on 23 May 1966, when he was Home Secretary, is relevant here: he said it was 'equal opportunity, accompanied by cultural diversity, in an atmosphere of mutual tolerance'.

Relationships with outsiders for the all-male group are limited. In the spheres of work and neighbourhood contacts tend to be slight, except with the population of women which will often be relatively mobile.[10] In a city like Bradford, the number of women and girls coming from outside is very high. Some are prostitutes, but others are girls absconding from approved schools and other institutions who are looking primarily for the anonymity and escape that may be available in the setting of the immigrant area or zone of transition. Immigrant areas, despite the relatively heavy concentration of police in them, are among those which offer the prospect of anonymity for people on the run.

Other kinds of relationships may require, and in fact get, an adaptation of behaviour. In some households with young men contacts may be made with the neighbours for various reasons. It may be that advice is required about a form to be filled in, or a neighbour, possibly elderly, decides to encourage the men to keep their garden tidy, or look after the outside of their house, washing windows or curtains or painting the woodwork. Some of these contacts have led to continuing friendships. There may be washing and ironing and mending done for the young men. All these contacts are quite unplanned. They do not happen everywhere but they can happen where the fabric of community life has not been swamped by the mobility which affects the majority, and where the pride in cleanliness and order, in face of the pollution in the centre of many towns and cities, implies more than just an inward-looking privatized life. Even relationships of this kind or the cameraderie of the public places where people meet involves only minor commitment.

Distinctions of a number of kinds have to be made, therefore, when considering the context of Muslim life in Britain. The settlements are in different stages. Some now (October 1968) will show a considerable diversity of age-groups, and a developing balance between the sexes among adults. Others, especially the relatively small settlements more recently settled, often as offshoots from elsewhere, may still be mainly all-male. Little research has been done on the ecological succession aspects of migration, and in particular the extent to which settlements in one area develop colonies in other areas. Information which is available about West Yorkshire shows, for example, that Bradford provided the main source of migrants for the settlements in smaller West Yorkshire towns such as Halifax, Keighley and, to a lesser extent, Dewsbury. The social structure of the larger areas will be more diverse and groups are more likely to be in a variety of settlements rather than one or two. More families are usually to be found in the larger settlements and in part this seems to arise because those moving to the smaller towns, at the second stage, are involved in more expense than those who stay in the same towns. This is not invariably true, as there is a good deal of mobility within areas of settlement anyway, but it appears to be a contributory factor. Certainly the number of schoolchildren in places more recently settled is fewer though the proportion is growing rapidly. In some towns in West Yorkshire the size of this entry group increased six times in the two years from 1965 to 1967.[11]

The organization of a community which is small may take much longer to arrange, particularly where a diversity of groups is represented. Where, however, there is a similarity in background, as for example, in a settlement which is almost entirely from the same small area of India or Pakistan and consists of people of the same religion, the structure of leadership can develop rapidly and all kinds of consequences can flow from this in terms of relationships between the newcomers and the local born. The attempt to create national organizations among Pakistanis has been bedevilled by factionalism, and those organizations of a formal kind which begin with social priorities (however they may broaden to meet other needs which emerge) remain stronger than those with overtly political ambitions.

There is a considerable difference between life in a relatively simple type of society, such as those in the areas from which immigrants from India and Pakistan come, and the complex setting of life in Britain. The pervading presence of the joint three-generational family is usually absent. In addition there are great differences between the ways in which families adapt in different areas of the country. Density of settlement and the extent to which other groups live in the same area may have a bearing on the kinds of leadership structure which develops and the extent to which the community becomes inward-looking and especially mindful of preserving its own ways of life, or outward-looking and prepared to make some kind of accommodation with the society outside it.

There appears to have been an assumption by some Muslims that women in Britain who did not cover their legs and the rest of the person in a way appropriate to the modesty of the Muslim women were of loose morals. Others extended this judgment to the normal situation in British towns whereby women were often seen walking about on their own, again something which would not happen in the villages of the Indian sub-continent. It is easy to see how a view of British society as immoral developed. The extent to which this happened varied considerably according to the individuals concerned – in some ways they may have been a means of allaying feelings of guilt for their own conduct – but its effect was perhaps in part designed to minimize any involvement in the society.

On the other hand the opportunities for a much more permissive line of conduct were available for men. Figures, for example, for venereal disease and the number of children born to local women and Pakistani fathers indicate that many were living with or otherwise involved with local-born women. The village organization which preserved in large part the faithfulness of the husband, in that he would associate with his brothers or other kinsfolk, was replaced by a situation in which individual autonomy and choice could become more important. Only a minority of men lived away from contacts with relatives, but some were quite marginal to the group and tended to go their own ways. Even those living with relatives shared the same kinds of frustrations arising from the absence of their wives and many came to accept and condone relationships which were formed with women living nearby. In some cases these liaisons were relatively stable and between one woman and one man, but in others one woman was shared between several men and may have lived in the same house.

Urban society provides the opportunity for anonymity and the exercise of personal preferences, but undoubtedly there were stresses for many Muslims because their conduct was at variance both with what they had been taught and how they had behaved in the village environment in the past. Removal of the informal social controls led to changes in patterns of life which made it difficult to envisage a return to the much more limited range of activities that were present in their countries of origin. From the kinship group protecting and preserving standards of appropriate behaviour in the village a movement took place whereby the same kinship group of men living in a lodging-house situation perhaps began by condoning the behaviour of one of their number and eventually participated in it.

Some marriages have taken place between local-born women and Muslims. Quite a large number of the girls who live with Muslim men seem to have gone through a ceremony of marriage which is not in fact legal in this country unless it is supplemented by a civil ceremony. Attitudes towards women may have to be modified to some extent in the new situation, particularly in the period of court-ship before 'marriage'. Moreover the area of freedom which these women have been used to will be much greater than that of the Muslim women. In such circumstances either the man may accept that his wife will never act in the same way as his mistress, or else his views about the role of the woman, and the participation which some of these women expect in day-to-day life, may be modified with various long-term effects in the future.

Some of the women involved, particularly those who marry in a way which is legal in this country, become indistinguishable from their Muslim counterparts, associating more or less exclusively with other women and adopting habits of deference and demureness in the presence of their husbands.

How far the families, and individuals within them, change varies considerably. Much may depend on the kind of environment in which they settle and the extent to which they have contact with the people living in the same area. A number of considerations apply here which have the effect of making adaptations more likely. Among these are the desire on the part of the man for a home for his family at some distance from the areas of all-male households.

In part this reflects his desire to keep his wife away from the possible consequences of contact with unattached males. If there is only a limited amount of housing available this may not be so possible and undoubtedly some families live in what are otherwise all-male settings and others are in houses which are in multi-occupation by people of different backgrounds. That the desire to keep a wife away from contact with other men is important is evidenced by the occasional cases of murder or serious injury which arise because of the jealousy of the husband or the involvement of the wife in relationships which could hardly arise in the secluded environment of the village in the country of origin.

Many families of Muslims appear to live some distance from the areas of all-male settlement, when the latter are a relatively high proportion of the group, if some housing choice is available. In addition some families, for various reasons, move further out into the suburbs when they come and may lose touch in many respects with the community as a whole. This mobility, either into private housing or more rarely into local authority housing, arises only for a small minority, but the reasons that take the families out from the centre include levels of aspiration which are quite similar to those experienced by British people generally. There is a stong sense of the importance of education among many Muslims, although this tends to be viewed as a means to high social status and economic opportunity rather than as an end in itself. Parents motivated in this way may come to realize that the quality of education relates to the environment in which the school is placed as well as to what is offered within it, and the desire to move arises. Once children are moved to a setting in which they are a small minority rather than one where they are a large and growing proportion of the school population, the chances of making friends across the ethnic divisions would seem to be increased. In the main this kind of mobility and these kinds of tendencies are exhibited to begin with by those of relatively high status. Doctors and other professional people tend to make this kind of move early on in their careers rather than stay in the areas mainly inhabited by fellow Muslims. Moreover the tradition in which they have lived in Pakistan will tend to make them behave very differently from the average peasant who provides the backbone of migration to Britain.

Commenting on the extent to which many Pakistanis of high social status observe the Muslim religion and its precepts, one

informant suggested that the attitude was one in which only lip
service was paid in general, whilst drinking and other deviations
were quite common in private. On the other hand few Muslims who
live in this way are prepared to be other than orthodox in public
situations. There is thus a gap between what is common behaviour
in private and what is professed at the public level. The distinctions
between those of lower status in these respects are less likely to have
arisen in the countries of origin but they are more likely to arise in
the British situation.

Ways of life at deviance with the acceptable code of conduct become
increasingly common, it is suggested, and there is an increasing
diversity among them. The consciousness of this fact leads to questions about leadership within the community which are not yet
resolved in most areas in which Muslims settle. Political life is
characterized by a good deal of factionalism in leadership, and
the acceptance of leaders is related to kinship and neighbourhood
groupings rather than anything on a wider scale. What emerges is
an often bitter struggle in which those with high status in the country
of origin are not necessarily those with high status, in terms of
economic success, in Britain. Some of the most successful businessmen may be only semi-literate and will in all likelihood have begun
as manual labourers in Britain. Conscious of the gap between their
economic power and their standing in the community, such men
may make bids for leadership. The Imams and other religious
leaders may be in a position to influence policies in a secular sphere
more than would have arisen in the countries of origin. In particular,
questions about dress and schoolchildren, and the whole matter of
the adherence to an acceptable Muslim way of life, involve some
religious leaders and make some of them aware of their potential
influence in the power structure of the community as a whole. Given
the changes in ways of life, and the guilt which many people feel in
consequence of this, some leaders are in a position to support the
religion and strict adherence to it by polarizing the interests of
minority group and host community.

One critic of Muslim society today, suggesting that the Muslim
world is ripe for the kind of upheaval that took place in Christendom
at the Reformation, has this to say about the contrast in several
religions between what is believed and the progress of knowledge:

It is terrifying to watch how religion, shackled by revelation, makes no effort to join in this ascent. It seems, on the contrary, to insist on continuing to advise men to fix their thoughts on a lifeless mould, to refrain from all reflection and discussion, and to content themselves with religious observances which confine twentieth-century believers within the circle of magic rites that circumscribed the lives of their remotest ancestors . . . Islam . . . is still dominated by the clerical spirit of the old class of *fuqaha*, the jurist theologians who have reduced its thought to the level of scholastic tittle-tattle.[12]

At least Islam is not ruled, in the view of the same writer, by a clergy in the grip of a routine of dogma and rite. The role of the Imam, however, can change between the country of origin and Britain. In the villages from which the great majority of Muslims in Britain come, the Imam is a person of importance. He is not usually well educated, except in his knowledge of the scriptures. He heads the community in prayers, gives lessons to the children, performs marriage ceremonies, leads funeral prayers and discusses the topic of the day in his sermon on a Friday.

In Britain the Imam has less respect in the community, at least initially. He acts as caretaker of the mosque if there is one, and may well live in a room there. If he cannot speak English he is not in a good position to act for the groups. There are many discussions among religious leaders about dress, diet and the teaching of Muslim children. A much stronger line against such things as short skirts for girls and mixed physical education and swimming has developed in some towns where an initially more permissive approach by some parents reflected a fluid leadership situation. In some cases Imams appear to have acquired considerable power, especially in terms of blocking change, but in others they act for the leadership of the community as a whole. What emerges is a narrow view of what is desirable in terms of accommodation, and a whole range of cultural features is involved.

There is much stronger emphasis within the family on the authority of its senior members and in particular of the father. In a society without social security and welfare the obligations of children to support parents are stressed. In the presence of parents the child must be docile and quiet, and a degree of formality develops in the relationships between fathers and sons as the sons get older. One aspect of this is the way in which fathers lay down what their children should do. In more permissive situations there is a conflict between what children from this background see as being the practice of their schoolfellows and their parents and what is expected of them at home. In addition there are great distinctions between the roles of men and women. Generalization is difficult because so much depends upon the personal circumstances of the individual, and women of a higher social group, especially if living in cities, have much more freedom than their rural counterparts. In Pakistan there is a discrepancy between the rights which women are accorded by the teachings of religion and their actual situation. Under Muslim law women have rights, for example, to inheritance and divorce, but there is a great discrepancy between what their situation is according to law and what it is in practice if they live in remote rural areas.

The activity of women is mainly confined to the domestic sphere. Men spend their leisure time with companions of their own sex and marriage is an alliance of families. Girls are protected, after puberty, from contact with men who are not related. When a girl marries she is expected to have had no contact with young men at all. One informant said, in contrasting British and Muslim practice:

> It is really unfortunate that even some teachers approach Muslim parents to allow their daughters to adopt the English way of life, such as having boy-friends, which is totally unacceptable to our culture.[13]

The kind of problems which arise in practice in the school situation include girls sitting next to boys and talking to them. In a Muslim society they cease to mix at an early age. Girls adopt traditional female dress which covers the legs and they remain in a secluded world. Any hint of irregular behaviour on the part of the girl, such as conversing with boys, may affect not only her marriage prospects but also those of her relatives.

The difficulties of preserving this degree of separation, and the institution of 'purdah', by which women are protected from contact with males outside their family circle, are obvious in Britain. At first some women were taken to clinics by their husbands but conflicts arise between the need for husbands to be at work and to protect their wives. Modifications of practice are inevitable in many cases and have taken place. Often women look upon the visit to the clinic or shops as an excursion. If possible they go with another woman, who is usually related.

Preserving dietary practices may also be difficult. Quite large numbers of Muslim men appear to drink alcohol, and it is not always possible to check where the foodstuffs come from and in particular whether meat is being killed in the approved way. Children who stay for school meals may be particularly liable to eat food which is not prepared according to precept.

In the sphere of education the demands of parents, or the conflicts between the values of the family and the values of the school, cause tensions for the child. One practical issue is that the desire to teach the child about Muslim culture and religion may mean that children, often quite young, spend long hours at the weekend or after school or both, learning about their traditions. Though not all children attend the classes which are provided there are increasing constraints to do so. However, if parents become aware of the strains which this is imposing they may well question the importance of traditional studies of their religion and culture as compared with the subjects taught in the school situation. Those with a strong motivation for their children to do well and adapt themselves and obtain better jobs may be more resistant to this development.

The methods employed by the teachers at the schools set up by the communities or groups are far more formal and authoritarian than those in an English school. The reverence for learning which is inculcated is one which is closely allied to and forms of rote learning rather than a critical assessment of the position. Thus even for the child in a good school environment problems of adaptation frequently arise and the teaching models reveal considerable differences between the situation in which he learns about his background and that in which he learns to adapt himself to English society. There is also the problem of the 'helpful' parent, teaching in a way alien to the tradition in this country. Parents adopting an inflexible, authoritarian attitude may well dominate their children and, for example, keep them within the confines of the home quite effectively, but in a number of cases there may well be open discontent and the possibility of family breakdown. To specify the kinds of breakdown which could arise, and put a relative value on them, would be difficult at this stage of the settlements, but undoubtedly delinquency is one possible area of deviation. Others include relationships with people of the same age group of the opposite sex. The fears in this respect are almost always expressed on behalf of the girls rather than the boys.

The changes going on in patterns of life and consequent effects on religious beliefs and cultural practices seem to be anticipated hardly at all by the Muslim community in Britain. On the whole the attitude of the religious leadership is to ignore the kinds of consequences that are likely to arise from life in a more affluent, sophisticated and urban environment. Some informants suggested that parents were aware of some of the considerable problems but hoped that they would not arise in an acute form in their own lifetime. Those in a position to make a choice and who move to the edges of the areas may well accommodate themselves to some aspects of life in Britain and obtain far more benefits both for themselves and for their children. On the other hand these are people in the front line of integration, as it were, and the response to them will depend on the general character of race relations in the country. Accommodation that does take place will reflect the growing similarity of interests, at least in certain respects, between migrants and native-born.

With increasing affluence and the extent to which the society remains, or becomes, more 'open' in terms of opportunities linked to ability, changes are more likely to take place. One of the more significant developments in recent years has been the emergence of a definite class structure which, professional people apart, is not entirely based on the working class. There are two main groups of the upwardly mobile. One is of those professional people in medicine or law who provide services both for the minority group and for the host community. The other, a much larger section, is of people who have begun as workers but, by dint of saving, have acquired business and commercial interests. The form this takes is either through the ownership of property or the ownership of shops. Styles of life in some cases may begin to approximate more closely to those of the equivalent groups in the host community. Many similarities exist between those who have emerged from the working class and those who have stayed in it, but it is conceivable that, for some, class and social group interests can outweigh the ethnic loyalties which previously have prevailed.

Not all will be influenced, especially in a situation where there is a high density of settlement. It is possible that the greater the concentration in the ghetto situation the more the need for a siege mentality will develop. At the same time great changes are likely to come about in traditional structures of authority. How far the Muslim religion can retain its hold in a completely different situation and in a modern society which has few similarities with those in which the majority of Muslims live is an open question.

There can be no certainty about what will happen in the future to the religious beliefs, practices and ways of life of Muslims in Britain. Some writers anticipate a strong conservative trend in the immediate future.[14] The character of British society is obviously of great importance. Its homogeneity must not be exaggerated. At the same time, as Banton notes:

> These implicit notions about the proper way to behave, about the unannounced rights and obligations of people in particular positions, constitute the unspoken language of British social life; . . . seen from this standpoint, strangers are people whose behaviour cannot be predicted or controlled.[15]

The temper of expressed public opinion has undoubtedly worsened recently, but at the same time the Race Relations Act of 1968 provides an earnest of the intention of reducing discrimination.

There are a number of factors which make forms of adaptation more or less likely. Amongst those which the Muslims bring with them which make for resistance to change is their particular religious and cultural system. In varying respects, as has been described, it creates points of conflict with the structure operating in the host society. There are not only different views but also different priorities in terms of such questions as relationships between the sexes and education. The factionalism of leadership could also result in factors which affect the security of the group. If these were coupled with threats from society outside it could lead, and there is evidence to suggest that this is happening, to an inward-looking structure. Awareness of restriction of opportunities arises less in the generation which settled in a particular country than it does for the second generation. If opportunities are restricted for the second-generation Muslims there will be less chance of a multi-racial adaptation developing.

Some of the more important factors making for change include the difficulties of religious observance at stated times because of occupational and other demands. The changing class structure could provide opportunities for identification on a social group rather than an ethnic basis. Other important considerations include the knowledge of other ways of life, derived from either observation or contact, or the mass media, and opportunities for increased prosperity and mobility. What happens will be the consequence of the interaction between the factors which make for change and those which inhibit it, in the varied context of life in Britain.

ACKNOWLEDGMENT

I have been fortunate in having the advice and assistance of many people in the preparation of this article. The interpretations of the material are my own, and would be unlikely to be acceptable to some of those I have consulted. For their courtesy and care in answering my questions I am particularly grateful to the following: R. El Droubie, E. Ul Haq, C. M. Revis, and R. Irtizaali.

NOTES

1. A useful introduction is to be found in F. Hashmi, *The Pakistan Family in Britain*, London: National Committee for Commonwealth Immigrants, 1966.

2. Kenneth Cragg, *The Call of the Minaret*, London: Oxford University Press, 1956, p. 106.

3. Z.H., 'Zikat for the Poor', *Morning News*, 18 October 1968, p. 11.

4. R. El Droubie, *A Muslim View of Jesus and Christianity* (Muslims in Britain, No. 1), London: Islamic Cultural Centre (duplicated), p. 23.

5. See G. E. Marrison, *The Christian Approach to the Muslim*, London: Edinburgh House Press, 1959, p. 30.

6. *The Guardian*, 4 November 1968.

7. M. Gaudefroy-Demombynes, *Muslim Institutions*, Eng. trans. by J. P. MacGregor, London: Allen and Unwin, 1950, pp. 71 f.

8. R. Desai, *Indian Immigrants in Britain*, London: Oxford University Press, 1963, p. 93.

9. Census, 1961, England and Wales: *Commonwealth Immigrants in the Conurbations*, London: HMSO, 1965.

10. See Eric Butterworth, *A Muslim Community in Britain*, London: Church Information Office, 1967.

11. See Eric Butterworth (ed.), *Immigrants in West Yorkshire*, London: Institute of Race Relations, 1967.

12. M. Gaudefroy-Demombynes, *op. cit.*, pp. 208 f.

13. Quoted in Butterworth, *A Muslim Community in Britain*, p. 44.

14. John Goodall: 'The Pakistani Background', in *New Backgrounds*, ed. Robin Oakley, London; Institute of Race Relations, 1968, p. 90.

15. Michael Banton, *Race Relations*, London: Tavistock Publications, 1967, p. 372.

9 Humanism in Britain: the Formation of a Secular Value-oriented Movement

Colin Campbell

HUMANISM AND THE BRITISH HUMANIST MOVEMENT

HUMANISM, interpreted as the general tendency to regard man as the measure of all things, is a philosophical attitude of great antiquity and can be identified in the cultures of many civilizations both past and present.[1] In the context of contemporary British society, however, Humanism is the name given to the ideology of the British Humanist Movement and although this ideology derives inspiration from the wide and ancient humanistic tradition, it is, like the movement with which it is associated, a distinctive creation of the mid-twentieth century. Some elements of Humanism have clearly been carried forward from the secular ideologies of a previous age. For example, the concentration of attention on 'this life' has been carried forward from the Secularism of George Jacob Holyoake, the focus on science and rationality from Rationalism and the emphasis on disinterested service of mankind from the Ethical Culture Movement. But other features of Humanism are very much the product of a fresh response to an altered environment.

The existential content of Humanism is primarily derived from that of science and correspondingly contains a view of the universe which is monistic, impersonal and lacking in intrinsic purpose though subject to evolution. Man is seen as unique in his capacity as the creator and bearer of culture and is the principal agent for further evolution on this planet.[2] The acceptance of this world-view is associated with the rejection of the Christian beliefs concerning God, immortality and original sin. The emotional response contained in Humanism is presented as a ready acceptance of the conditions of human life whilst the primary moral commitment consists of a responsibility for mankind. Within this general framework of belief the goal value of Humanism is given as 'human fulfilment' and the primary instrumental values as scientific knowledge and service. Other secondary and derived values include those of reason, disinterestedness, pluralism, freedom of speech and anti-authoritarianism. Governing the expression of these values there is in the humanist *Weltanschauung* a spirit of optimism and a practical orientation to life.

The British Humanist Movement consists of those organizations which have an explicit commitment to this value-orientation. Some of these organizations were created expressly to promote Humanism, whilst others developed a humanist commitment out of an existing commitment to another culture-system. In this latter case the 'conversion' to Humanism has not always been complete. There exists, therefore, a range of organizations from those which are wholly humanist, through those which possess a humanist commitment in varying degrees, to those which are not humanist in their commitment.

National organizations which are unequivocally humanist in character are the British Humanist Association (formerly the Ethical Union) and the Student Humanist Federation (formerly the University Humanist Federation). Also clearly humanist in their commitment are the local groups which describe themselves as humanist and have been formed since 1954–5. The majority of these are in fact affiliated to one or other of the above national bodies. An organization which is predominantly humanist in character although retaining something of its earlier distinctive commitment to Rationalism is the Rationalist Press Association. Most local ethical societies and the more than local South Place Ethical Society have also adopted Humanism, although the flavour of the earlier commitment often remains. Most recently the National Secular Society has begun to blend Humanism in with its traditional commitment to secularism.[3]

These national and local organizations jointly constitute the British Humanist Movement. Liaison between these bodies is not formalized, however, and joint action on matters of common interest therefore occurs irregularly. It is the British Humanist Association which usually acts as the principal spokesman for the movement.

The first clear sign of the emergence of a British Humanist Movement came in 1954 and 1955. Several local groups were formed in those two years by the Ethical Union, groups which soon styled themselves 'humanist' and which owed little to the ethical culture tradition which had inspired the Union itself. The success of these groups encouraged the Union to attempt to form more and the new groups became affiliated to the Union alongside the few remaining ethical societies. By 1957 the Rationalist Press Association had begun to advertise for members in the name of Humanism and the two organizations began a move towards closer collaboration. This move culminated in the creation of the British Humanist Association in 1963. The University Humanist Federation had been formed four years earlier through the initiative of an Oxford undergraduate and with the active support of both the Ethical Union and the Rationalist Press Association.

The rapidity of the growth of the Humanist Movement and its present extent is indicated in the following Table, which shows the growth in the number of local humanist groups since they first appeared in 1954 and 1955.

HUMANIST GROUPS IN EXISTENCE
1954–67

1954 (December)	4
1955 ,,	7
1956 ,,	9
1957 ,,	14
1958 ,,	15
1959 ,,	24
1960 ,,	30
1961 ,,	34
1962 ,,	31
1963 ,,	33
1964 (May)	45
1965 (April)	65
1966 (May)	75
1967 (December)	91

(These figures exclude Ethical Societies and University Groups).

Sources: *Humanist News* (News and Notes) and BHA Annual Reports.

THE BRITISH HUMANIST ASSOCIATION

The British Humanist Association was formed in 1963 as a 'common front organization' for the Ethical Union and the Rationalist Press Association and thus represented the recognition of the common interest in Humanism which these two bodies had developed in the preceding years.[4] Whilst a complete merger of the two organizations was prevented by the continuing commitment of the Rationalist Press Association to a distinctly rationalist position, the 'common front' arrangement prevented any unnecessary competition in the name of Humanism. The Association took over all responsibility for publicity and advertising in the name of Humanism, promoted humanist publications, organized conferences and acted as a pressure group in furthering humanist interests in social reforms, education, broadcasting and the press. The Association proved to be a considerable success, receiving approximately 4,000 enquiries in the first eight months of its existence. By April, 1965, two years after its formation, it had an individual membership of 2,898 and 65 affiliated local groups.[5] It was by this time regarded by members and non-members alike as the premier organization in the British Humanist Movement, although its constitutional position remained that of a 'common front' organization.

In July, 1965, the Ethical Union was removed from the register of charities by the Charity Commissioners.[6] This decision not only presented the Union with the threat of an annual deficit of £3,000 due to the loss of tax rebate but also caused the British Humanist Association to be removed from the register since its aims included those of the Ethical Union. Although the Ethical Union appealed against the decision, the immediate result was to destroy the existing structure of the British Humanist Association since it had become legally improper for the Rationalist Press Association (itself a charity) to continue to support a non-charitable body (the BHA). The RPA therefore withdrew its support and interim arrangements for continuing the work of the BHA were implemented whilst new plans for the Association were considered.[7]

The immediate effect of this sudden and unforeseen destruction of the existing organizational structure of the Humanist Movement was to give a very real significance to an existing debate about the movement's primary task. The Union had lost its charitable status because its aims could be interpreted as implying political activity, but when the suggestion was made that the aims should be altered so that charitable status could be regained, the objection was raised that this was 'risking preventing effective Humanist participation in political affairs'.[8] Since the educational and propaganda aims of Humanism were clearly fitted to a charitable body the question of whether the

BHA should be a charity or not raised the question of whether socio-political aims or educational-propaganda aims were the primary concern of the movement. An additional complication was added by the fact that the RPA had only recently acquired charitable status at considerable legal expense and thus had no intention of becoming a non-charitable organization. Therefore, the choice of non-charitable status would mean that the EU (BHA) would have to go on alone, whilst if charitable status was obtained the EU and RPA could once again jointly sponsor the BHA.

An Extraordinary General Meeting of the EU (BHA) on 14 January, 1967 decided by an overwhelming majority of members (996 to 12) not to seek to regain charitable status. This meeting also approved the change of name of the Ethical Union to the British Humanist Association, and established new legal objects. In addition, a decision was taken to make 1967 a Campaign Year for the Association in an effort to recruit new members and so help offset the financial loss involved in the permanent loss of charitable status.[9] The way was therefore cleared for the new, reorganized, BHA to prepare a programme of action for Humanism, based on the general principles of the humanist value-orientation but specifying particular social and political objectives. This was done at the annual conference in July, 1967, when a general statement of policy was adopted and a five-year plan approved.[10]

The BHA had concerned itself with social issues ever since its formation in 1963 and had indeed issued policy documents on those of most concern to humanists. The new non-charitable con-stitution, however, gave a fresh impetus to this form of activity and the first annual conference under this constitution was given over entirely to policy-making. The immediate result of this was the formulation of *A General Statement of Policy*, a document of thirty-three items under thirteen headings and outlining in general terms the humanist position on a very wide range of topics including 'International Relations, War and Disarmament'; 'The Arts, Leisure and Man's Physical Environment'; 'Religion in Society'; and 'Economics, Wages Policy and Social Insurance'. Other areas covered included Health and the Social Services, World Population and Resources, the Shape of Society, Parliamentary and Political Reform, Education, The Law and Morality, Censorship, Crime and Penal Policy, Racial Discrimination, Civil Liberties and Science.[11]

In addition to formulating a general statement of humanist policy,

F

the BHA annual conference of 1967 also established specific objectives for itself for the following five years. These were as follows:

The abolition of the act of worship and religious instruction in county schools in favour of social and moral education.

The elimination of areas where the only maintained school available is a denominational one.

The ending of the entrenched position of religion in broadcasting, and revision of the religious clauses in the charter of ITA and the allocation of much more broadcasting time to the discussion of Humanism.

The abolition of all forms of governmental subsidy for religious bodies.

The substitution of affirmation for oath-taking.

The taking up by all local authorities of the powers to act as adoption agencies given to them by Act of Parliament.[12]

DISCUSSION

The British Humanist Movement is a secular value-oriented movement. That is, it comes within Smelser's definition of a value-oriented movement as 'a collective attempt to restore, protect, modify, or create values in the name of a generalized belief'.[13] Humanism is just such a generalized belief or value-orientation, constituting as it does a conception of 'nature, man's place in it, man's relation to man, and the desirable and non-desirable as they may relate to man-environment and interhuman relations'.[14] At the same time, Humanism is secular rather than religious in character since super-empirical or non-empirical beliefs are deliberately excluded. A secular value-oriented social movement thus represents an attempt by members of a society to reconstruct individuals and society in accordance with an empirically based generalized belief. Such a movement is contrasted not only with religious value-oriented movements but with norm-oriented movements, the latter constituting attempts to 'restore, protect, modify, or create norms in the name of a generalized belief'.[15]

Since the distinction between value-oriented movements and norm-oriented movements rests primarily on the analytical distinction between values and norms, the identification of any particular social movement as either one or the other requires some qualification. In addition, values are components of social action of a more general character than norms, and so whilst a value-oriented movement can include demands for the reform of certain norms, the reverse is not likely to be the case.

The British Humanist Movement, as represented by the British Humanist Association, comprises a value-oriented movement which is affiliated to several norm-oriented movements. The BHA has close ties with such norm-oriented movements as the United Nations Association, the Howard League for Penal Reform, the National Council for Civil Liberties and most of all, with the Abortion Law Reform Association.[16] These organizations can be identified as norm-oriented movements independent of any value-oriented movement, not only because of their separate organization but more significantly because they do not query the legitimate value-structure of society, but rather derive support from it.[17] For this reason they are able to secure support from Christians who adhere to these values as well as from humanists who do not. Thus these movements to reform established legal norms can be distinguished from the similar attempts which are made *within* the humanist movement, such as the substitution of affirmation for oath-taking and the abolition of the act of worship in schools, as outlined in the BHA five-year plan. These demands for normative change follow from the denial of legitimacy to the established values and thus presuppose the existence of challenging values and a value-oriented movement.[18]

If this identification of the British Humanist Movement as value-oriented is correct, then it should be possible to apply Smelser's general theory of collective behaviour in an effort to identify the combination of determinants which eventuated in the formation and growth of the movement. This theoretical framework envisages value-oriented movements as one of five main types of collective behaviour (the panic, the craze, the hostile outburst, the norm-oriented movement and the value-oriented movement) which can collectively be regarded as uninstitutionalized attempts to reconstitute the social situation. In order to explain the occurrence of collective behaviour in general and its manifestation in any one or more of the above types, social action is broken down into its components (viz: values, norms, mobilization of motivation and situational facilities) and related to the major determinants of such behaviour in a 'value-added' process. The major determinants are identified as structural conduciveness, strain, crystallization of a generalized belief, precipitating factors, mobilization for action and social control. These determinants operate as a value-added process so that:

> Each determinant is a necessary condition for the next to operate as a determinant in an episode of collective behaviour. As the necessary conditions accumulate, the explanation of the episode becomes more determinate. Together the necessary conditions constitute the sufficient condition for the episode.[19]

The accumulation of these conditions is viewed as an analytical rather than a temporal sequence.

Structural Conduciveness.   This term refers to the degree to which any given socio-cultural structure permits one type of collective behaviour. In this context it refers to the extent to which the social and cultural structure of British society encourages value-oriented movements whilst discouraging other forms of collective behaviour. It is clear that an important element 'conducive' to the formation of such movements is the institutionalization in British society of the system of denominational pluralism. This system enables new value-oriented movements (typically movements of religious schisms in Protestant Christianity) to develop without becoming a threat to the legitimacy of the political constitution. This mechanism for the 'institutionalized insulation' of value-oriented movements represents conditions conducive to the development of dissenting movements, as it fosters an attitude of toleration towards movements representing 'variant' value-orientations.[20]   The   system   of   denominational pluralism however does not extend to a system of religious (including non-religious) pluralism but exists in British society within a context in which Christianity has the position of an established religion. This fact has implications concerning the degree to which British society is conducive to the formation of secular value-oriented movements like Humanism.

Societal value systems have been classified as either 'prescriptive' or 'principial' in type depending on whether they demand commitment to 'a vast range of relatively specific norms governing almost every situation in life' which is typically the case in traditional societies, or whether commitment is demanded to certain basic principles of social action but no attempt is made to regulate all specific social situations in detail, as is typically the case in modern society.[21] These two types of value system specify different relationships between the system of values and the differentiated systems of norms. In the former case any dispute over norms necessarily leads to a conflict of values; as Bellah suggests, small changes in any sphere are likely to involve supernatural sanctions.[22] In the latter case, however, the relative autonomy of economic, political and social life means that norms can largely be determined by situational and functional considerations and any conflict over norms is not likely to lead directly to a clash of values. The relevance of this distinction to the problem of structural conduciveness for value-oriented movements is that a 'prescriptive' value system is conducive to such movements since any attempt to restructure norms will lead directly to a conflict of values. A 'principial' value system on the other hand allows for normative reform without 'bringing matters to a head' in a clash of values; such a system does not therefore 'push' norm-oriented movements into value-oriented ones.

Although the value system of contemporary British society is clearly more principial than prescriptive in character, it does retain some features of the latter type, and these arise from the fact of Christianity's position as an established religion. Thus there are social situations in the fields of education, medicine, law and broadcasting (for example) where adherence to specific norms is directly associated with commitment to a generalized non-denominational Christianity. A move to query or restructure these norms therefore is likely to spill over into a conflict of values because of their prescriptive quality. This structural feature thus inhibits the formation of purely norm-oriented movements to express dissatisfaction with such social situations, whilst facilitating the move to the higher level component of social action represented by values.

Strain. This term is used to refer to the impairment of the relations among parts of a system and the consequent malfunctioning of the system, and, as Smelser observes, 'some structural strain must be present for one or more types of collective behaviour to occur'.[23] Two sources of strain can be identified as relevant to the formation of the British Humanist Movement. The first, which can be said to fall under the very general heading of 'role strain' arises from the prescriptive element in the value-system of society indicated above.

This element places a limit on the autonomy of certain spheres of social life, so that, to take the most obvious example, the sphere of education is not completely free to adapt its norms in accord with purely educational values but must take some as 'given' by the established religious values of society. This means that there is a possibility that the teacher will experience a conflict between the norm (which has a religious and not educational legitimation) and his commitment to educational values. Such a conflict could clearly be a source of strain, especially when the teacher has little or no religious commitment.[24] Other professionals, however, may experience strain for similar reasons, as for example a similar situation existed until recently for doctors in relation to the law relating to abortion which represented a similar religiously legitimated norm in a largely autonomous sphere, that of medicine. This form of strain seems to arise from the fact that social norms have not kept pace with changing social conditions, so that for a section of the population at least, the norms no longer conform to their expectations.

Strain of a different kind can also be identified as helping to provide a dynamic for the humanist movement. This is cultural strain, an impairment in the relations between the elements which comprise the cultural definitions institutionalized in society. At a very general level there is a discontinuity between the two major cultural traditions of science and religion, and to a lesser extent between art and science. This has in turn led to a reconsideration of fundamental justificatory beliefs and the basis of legitimation of action. It is not surprising that the formation of a new value-orientation should be one response to such strain.

Crystallization of a General Belief.   The existence of a generalized belief is recognized as essential for any episode of collective behaviour, and its function can be stated as follows:

> Before collective action can be taken to reconstitute the situation brought on by structural strain, this situation must be made meaningful to the potential actors. This meaning is supplied in a generalized belief, which identifies the source of strain, attributes certain characteristics to this source, and specifies certain responses to the strain as possible or appropriate.[25]

It can be seen without much difficulty that Humanism fulfils these functions in relation to the above stated forms of strain. The conflict between science and religion is removed by the rejection of the supernatural and the adoption of monism, whilst the philosophical basis of science is taken as the basis of all knowledge. A basis for morality is sought in the concept of human fulfilment. The experience of role strain is explained in terms of the illegitimate demands of religion and the reform of norms with purely religious justification is specified as the appropriate response. The crystallization of Humanism as a generalized belief can be regarded as a syncretism of cultural elements, some derived from preceding value-orientations like Secularism, Rationalism and Ethical Culture and others derived from the cultural traditions of certain professions.[26]

Precipitating Factors

A precipitating factor is an event that creates, sharpens, or exaggerates a condition of strain or conduciveness. It provides adherents of a belief with more evidence of the workings of evil forces, or greater promise of success. A precipitating factor, then, links the generalized belief to concrete situations, and thus brings the movement closer to actualization.[27]

More than one such precipitating factor can be identified as having contributed to the emergence of Humanism and the formation of a humanist movement. One of the earliest of these was the broadcasting in February, 1955 of two talks by Margaret Knight on the subject of 'Morals Without Religion'. Her direct presentation of an essentially humanist position created an uproar in the national press and can certainly be said to have 'sharpened' the cultural and structural strain attendant on a conflict between religious and non-religious commitment. The fact of her broadcast and the associated publicity also provided an impetus to the emerging humanist movement whilst contributing to the 'crystallization' of the generalized belief of Humanism. Another precipitating factor which helped to 'actualize' the movement was the holding of the second International Congress of the Humanist and Ethical Union in London in July, 1957. This not only provided another opportunity of bringing Humanism to the notice of the general public but was the occasion for a sustained advertising campaign on behalf of the Rationalist Press Association. In a similar way the BHA's loss of charitable status in 1965 can be seen as a factor which 'precipitated' a sense of urgency in the movement and led directly to a new programme for the movement and the decision to hold a campaign year.

Mobilization for Action. This term is used by Smelser to refer to the actual commencement of the episode of collective behaviour in which the affected group is brought into action.[28] It therefore marks the commencement of a social movement. At the initial stages of the formation of such a movement one or more persons must supply leadership. Most studies of the nature of leaderships characterizing value-oriented movements have stressed the importance of charismatic leaders as agents of mobilization. However, it has been observed that

> In so far as a value-oriented movement receives material aid from outside sources, and in so far as it inherits an organizational structure, the need for charismatic leaderships lessens.[29]

Both these qualifications apply to the humanist movement and may thus help to explain the absence of charismatic leaders. In the initial phase of the humanist movement, between 1955 and 1963, the Ethical Union and the Rationalist Press Association provided the general organizational structure for the movement to develop. Since then the Ethical Union has transformed itself completely into a humanist organization. Both bodies also gave assistance to other humanist organizations, such as local groups and the University Humanist Federation, during their difficult early stages.

It is suggested that once a social movement has overcome the initial problems of mobilization in the incipient phase, it then passes into a phase of enthusiastic mobilization, followed by the period of institutionalization and organization.[30] If the incipient phase of the humanist movement is regarded as the period 1955–63, then the period since 1963 is clearly a period of 'enthusiastic mobilization'.[31] It is perhaps too early to tell whether the movement has yet passed from this phase into the phase of institutionalization and organization.

Social Control. This final determinant in the series is really a generic term for all the possible counter-determinants which prevent, interrupt, deflect, or inhibit the accumulation of the determinants considered above.[32] Thus it covers both the social controls which minimize the structural conduciveness and strain and thus help to prevent the occurrence of the social movement and those social controls which operate after the movement has been formed in an attempt to halt it or diminish its influence. In general, the many actions of established authorities towards the humanist movement have, since the nineteen-fifties, covered both 'responsiveness' – that is a readiness to listen to the grievances of the movement and to act on them – and 'inflexibility' – a refusal to consider grievances and an insistence on adherence to established norms and values. The resultant ambiguity has strengthened rather than weakened the experience of strain for those most affected. Thus the BBC allowed Margaret Knight's broadcast (out of ignorance of the possible consequences rather than policy), then reacted to public pressure after the ensuing uproar by not allowing humanists to present their views uncontested. Then the BBC changed its policy and decided to allow humanists to present their views. This inconsistency on the part of authorities is also experienced by individual humanists, some of whom encounter 'responsive' education authorities, headmasters, judges, hospital matrons and adoption societies, whilst others encounter equally 'inflexible' ones. It seems highly likely that this pattern of ambiguous responses from the representatives of authority does less to 'prevent, interrupt, deflect, or inhibit' the movement than a consistent policy of either responsiveness or inflexibility. Since the occurrence of responsiveness is uncertain it is likely to do little to reduce strain whilst the occurrence of inflexibility sharpens the strain and thus accentuates the demands of the movement.

The above determinants of a value-oriented movement are related in Smelser's theory in a value-added process, each determinant being the necessary condition for the next one in the series to operate. Thus, to work backward through the process: the British Humanist Movement actually came into existence as a direct result of the action 'mobilized' by the officials of the Ethical Union and the Rationalist Press Association (in conjunction with individual humanists). This mobilization of action, however, was only possible as a result of the sharp focusing of attention on the fundamental conditions of cultural and social strain provided by certain 'precipitating factors' both internal and external to the movement. Margaret Knight's broadcasts, the IHEU Congress in 1957 and the EU's loss of charitable status would seem to have fulfilled this function. It would not have been possible, however, to have focused attention on the fundamental conditions of strain without a generalized belief capable of identifying and explaining the strain and placing it in a larger context of meaning. This belief was provided by Humanism, a general value-orientation and associated belief which was the product of cultural syncretism and rationalization. The general dynamic for the episode of collective behaviour which resulted in the Humanist Movement arose from certain general conditions of strain existing in the socio-cultural system of British society. Strain in the social system existed mainly at the role level and was experienced by role occupants as a conflict between religiously sanctioned norms and occupational or social values. At the cultural level, strain was manifest between the world-views of science and religion. This source of strain, however, would not have manifest itself in a value-oriented social movement if the containing social structure had not been conducive. The British tradition of denominational pluralism meant that value-oriented movements were not discouraged, whilst the remaining 'prescriptive' quality of the established value-system of British society pushed the emerging movement of protest into a protest against values as well as against norms. The attitude of authority towards the emergent movement has been ambiguous, the demands of individual humanists and the movement having been met with both responsiveness and inflexibility at different times. This overall inconsistency has tended to negate any particular attempts to control the growth of the movement.

Only further research will show how accurate this summary account is as an explanation of the formation of the British Humanist Movement. Its adequacy, however, is circumscribed. The theory of collective behaviour employed above is a theory which tries to explain (*a*) why an episode of collective behaviour occurred, and (*b*) why it took the form it did (i.e., panic, craze, etc.). In this context the theory provides an answer to both questions and thus fulfils a useful role. It does not provide an explanation of why the *particular* form of value-oriented movement occurred. Thus it would be necessary to refer to another theory to account for the commitment to Humanism which distinguished this movement. Even within the limits of its explanatory power, however, Smelser's theory poses problems which invite further exploration. It is not clear, for example, exactly how the fact of social and cultural strain causes individuals to be motivated to join a social movement or why other individuals should be prepared to supply leadership. A more detailed account of the social-psychological processes involved in the creation of social movements is required. Also, it would appear that the concept of 'value-added' does not successfully perform its function of adequately specifying the complex relationships between the various 'determinants'. As has been suggested, the value-added model does not allow full recognition of

the complex, ongoing systemic process within which any one of the so-called 'necessary conditions' may in fact require for its generation the presence of one, two, or all of the other 'necessary conditions' to some degree—in a spiral, for example, of positive feedback.[33]

NOTES

1. M. Knight, *Humanist Anthology*, London: Barrie and Rockcliff, 1961.

2. For an exposition of this humanist cosmology see the writings of Sir Julian Huxley, especially *Religion without Revelation*, London: Max Parrish, 1957; *New Bottles for New Wine*, London: Chatto and Windus, 1957; *The Human Crisis*, Seattle: University of Washington Press, 1963; *Essays of a Humanist*, London: Chatto and Windus, 1964 (Penguin Books, 1966).

3. In a recent article entitled 'The Humanist Societies: the Consequences of a Diffuse Belief System', in *Patterns of Sectarianism*, ed. Bryan R. Wilson, London: Heinemann, 1967, Susan Budd does not distinguish between these organizations in terms of their differential commitment to Humanism. For a critique of this position see Colin B. Campbell, 'Strange Bedfellows', in *Humanist*, June 1968.

4. *The British Humanist Association* (pamphlet), not dated.

5. *Second Annual Report of the Committee*, The British Humanist Association, June, 1965.

6. *Third Annual Report of the Committee*, The British Humanist Association, July, 1966.

7. *Humanist News*, February-March, 1966.

8. *Humanist News*, September, 1965, p. 4.

9. *Humanist News*, February, 1967, p. 1.

10. *Humanist News*, September, 1967, p. 3.

11. *General Statement of Policy*, British Humanist Association, not dated.

12. *Humanist News*, September, 1968, p. 4.

13. N. J. Smelser, *Theory of Collective Behaviour*, London: Routledge and Kegan Paul, 1962. p. 313.

14. C. Kluckhohn, 'Values and Value-Orientations', in T. Parsons and E. A. Shils (eds.), *Toward a General Theory of Action*, Cambridge, Mass.: Harvard University Press, 1951; London: Oxford University Press, 1952, p. 411. Quoted by Smelser, p. 25.

15. Smelser, *op. cit.*, p. 270.

16. *Fourth Annual Report of the BHA*, July, 1967.

17. Smelser, p. 119.

18. For an interesting discussion of another British social movement in these terms, see R. Robertson, 'The Salvation Army: the Persistence of Sectarianism', in *Patterns of Sectarianism*, pp. 63-4.

19. Smelser, *op. cit.*, p. 382.

20. Smelser, *op. cit.*, p. 336.

21. R. N. Bellah, 'Religious Aspects of Modernization in Turkey and Japan', *American Journal of Sociology* 64.1, 1958, pp. 1-2.

22. Bellah, *art. cit.*, p. 2.

23. Smelser, *op. cit.*, p. 49.

24. The fact that this is an important source of strain in connection with the humanist movement is borne out by the importance given to reform of the present situation concerning religion in schools by the BHA and the high proportion of teachers who are members of the Association. See Colin B. Campbell, 'Membership Composition of the British Humanist Association', *The Sociological Review*, New Series, 13.3, 1965, pp. 327-337.

25. Smelser, *op. cit.*, p. 16.

26. This argument is developed further in C. B. Campbell, *Humanism and the Culture of the Professions: A Study of the Rise of the British Humanist Movement 1954-63*, Ph.D. Thesis, University of London, 1967.

27. Smelser, *op. cit.*, p. 352.

28. Smelser, *op. cit.*, p. 17.

29. Smelser, *op. cit.*, p. 356.
30. Smelser, *op. cit.*, p. 298.
31. See Table on p. 159.
32. Smelser, *op. cit.*, p. 17.
33. W. Buckley, *Sociology and Modern Systems Theory*, Englewood Cliffs: Prentice Hall, 1967, p. 73.

10 The Christian-Communist Rapprochement: Some Sociological Notes and Questions[1]

Alasdair MacIntyre

IN RECENT years there has been a degree of discussion and rapprochement between Christians and Communists that could not have been predicted even ten years ago. At Salzburg in 1965, Herrenchiemsee in Bavaria in 1966 and Marianske Lazne in Czechoslovakia in 1967 congresses which had both papal (although both Protestants and Catholics were involved) and party approval were held. Roger Garaudy's conciliatory *De l'Anathème au Dialogue: un Marxiste s'adresse au Concile*[2] has its counterpart in a good deal of Christian writing. In England *Marxism To-Day*, the Communist Party's monthly journal, published fourteen articles, which have since appeared as *Dialogue of Christianity and Marxism*,[3] and a conference has been held between the British Council of Churches and the editorial board of *Marxism To-Day*. There have also been important discussions in Italy.

In the perspective of the history of their relationship or lack of it this dialogue between Christians and Communists is scarcely the natural and inevitable occurrence which the tone of much of the discussion seems to suggest. Why it should have occurred at all, and why it has occurred as and when and where it has are matters which clearly require some explanation. In this paper I make a first attempt to sketch the possible outlines for such an explanation. I do this by first noting some extremely peculiar factors of the rapprochement and suggesting a sociological explanation of these features. But since I am opening up areas of enquiry that are relatively new, I am also forced to reflect upon the theoretical issues raised by this attempt at exploration. Hence the second section of this paper. In the third section I try to bring these reflections to bear on the empirical facts summarized in the first section.

I

The most obvious oddity in the recent Christian-Communist conversations has been the readiness of each side to present a highly eccentric version of their own beliefs and to accept from the other side as authentic an equally eccentric version of theirs. On the Marxist side the eccentricity has had two distinguishing features. There has been first of all a radical departure from the view of Christianity held by Marx and Engels, and by Lenin and Kautsky too for that matter. Marx and Engels, wrote of an earlier attempt by Christians to enlist on the Left:

> Christian socialism is but the holy water with which the priest consecrates the heartburning of the aristocrat.

Contrast with this not merely the attitudes, but above all the emollient tone of M. Roger Garaudy when he writes:

> The future of man cannot be constructed in opposition to believers nor without them . . .

Garaudy's conciliationism has been sharply attacked by Althusser at a meeting of the Central Committee of the French Communist Party; but it is Garaudy's success in maintaining his stance in the face of such attacks which is significant. Garaudy argues that Marx's criticism of religion only applies to religion at certain phases of historical development and not to religion as such. But it was of course religion as such which Marx saw as an illusion generated by the miseries of class society.

As in the French discussions, so in the English. Dr John Lewis has used Marx's point against the Left Hegelians that the intellectual criticism of religion will not destroy belief, but that only a change in the social structures in which belief is rooted will do so, to suggest that Marx opposed direct attacks on religion. But to make this point in the interest of what is fashionably called dialogue between Marxists and Christians is at the very least a *suggestio falsi*. Certainly Marx followed Feuerbach in believing that religion had a human content of aspiration which would be achieved in real and not in illusory, that is, in religious form under Communism. But there is not a trace of a belief in Marx that any value at all attaches to the religious forms or that believers have any role to play, *qua* believers, in constructing the future.

The second way in which the version of Marxism presented by the

Communists to the Christians is eccentric to the Marxist tradition is a matter of the stress laid on such themes as alienation and the ideals to be realized in Communist society at the expense of such themes as class-struggle. Engels and Lenin, in the perspective of these conversations, are tiny figures compared with the Marx of 1844. One consequence of this is that the Marxist position has little concrete and specific about it; it is made into something general and moralistic. This is particularly evident when Garaudy is looking for common ground with Christians and finding it in Teilhard de Chardin. What he acclaims in Teilhard is the belief in the autonomy of science and the moral optimism. But of course such beliefs have flourished at many points in bourgeois society; when Marxists are driven to find common ground with Christians in the vulgar progressivism of Teilhard, they have left themselves little in common with Marx.

It would be too easy to suggest that the invocation of Teilhard is by itself evidence for the eccentric version of Christianity which is being propagated in these conversations. What is more important is that intellectually serious theologians such as Karl Rahner from the Catholic side and Jürgen Moltmann from the Protestant are involved in rewriting Christianity in ways that are far more subtle. Rahner and Moltmann alike emphasize that God is not an otherworldly king; Rahner takes him to be somehow the 'absolute future' of mankind and Moltmann, writing of the biblical God, is prepared to accept Ernst Bloch's characterization of him as one 'whose essential nature is the future'. The freedom of which the gospel speaks is taken to be the freedom of a future in which privilege is done away with. This emphasis on futurity is completely new in orthodox Christian theology. The New Testament is not oriented to the future, but to the Last Things. Yet such an interpretation of Christianity is not new. The name of Ernst Bloch ought to remind us of a tradition that goes back to Hegel, a tradition to which I have already alluded, according to which Christianity conceals in its religious formulas human truths which philosophical criticism of those formulas may disclose. Ernst Bloch in particular argued that Christianity has masked a Utopian hope for the future; but in arguing this, Bloch was never taken to be, and did not take himself to be, expounding orthodoxy. The 'this-worldly' interpretation of Christianity from Hegel and Feuerbach to Bloch was based on the view that atheism is true and theism false – in any ordinary sense of

these words. But now Moltmann transmutes belief in the Last
Things and belief in God into belief in a future of a certain kind.

Moltmann is a sophisticated theologian. What happens when the
same thesis is expressed without sophistication is a simple equation
of the key terms of Marxism with those of Christianity in which the
distinctive meaning belonging to both is lost.

> This, generally, is the perspective that christians share with marxists: for both,
> history proceeds in these three broad stages, moving from a primitive com-
> munity, through an era of destructive and serialized freedoms, to a reinte-
> gration of these freedoms in community. The liturgy is a symbolic – and thus
> genuine – surpassment of alienation, in precisely Marx's sense.[4]

Not, of course, true; but what I want to underline is the extreme
generality and lack of concreteness in this statement, a characteristic, it turns out, of both parties to this encounter. This generality,
this divesting of Christian and Marxist doctrines of their specific and
antagonistic character, does of course rest on something real. There
is a genuine historical relationship between Christianity and Marxism, mediated by Hegel and Feuerbach. But the contemporary
rapprochement makes claims which this historical relationship just
will not sustain, claims sometimes to a substantial identity between
Christian and Communist doctrine, as above, or claims as to a
possible synthesis of them in the future. We may also note that
divested of its transcendental character Christianity, too, becomes
moralistic and moralizing.

The two other features of these conversations worthy of special
remark are suggested by the first. The lack of concrete reference is
accompanied by a stress on consistency and inconsistency rather
than and at the expense of a concern with truth and falsity. At
Marianske Lazne Iring Fetscher drew attention to the failure of
Marx's key predictions and Paul Matussek, the Munich psycholo-
gist, reported on empirical work done on the reactions of persons
holding strong ideological beliefs to concentration camp experiences.
(What determined their reaction was the strength of the believer
rather than the particular content of the ideology.) But what those
particular contributions most strikingly revealed was the detachment of both Marxist and Christian positions from what ought for
them to have been key empirical facts. By 'detachment' I refer to the
ability of both parties to find some reasons for refraining from
radical modification or even abandonment of their positions in the
face of facts *prima facie* inconsistent with those positions. But it is

not only of course a matter of the inability of each side to engage in radical self-questioning about truth and falsity; it is also remarkable that neither side apparently felt the need to press the necessity for such questioning upon the other. Fetscher at Marianske Lazne seems never to have been able to press home his point about Marx's predictions; and at other conferences attempts to raise questions about actual events in Communist countries have failed. Of course it is true that the relation of Marxism to empirical facts is a complex one; Marxists always and rightly emphasize that the way we categorize and characterize the facts is in part at least determined by our general standpoint. But there are some key points at which Marxism is clearly testable; for one thing Marxist theory does claim predictives power. So Christianity too is related to the empirical facts in certain ways; the claim that Jesus Christ rose from the dead, the claim that he shall come again with glory, and the claim that it is possible for believers to lead a certain kind of life on earth are all empirical claims. The importance of this point will appear later; for the moment I want simply to note the absence of any effective Marxist critique of these Christian claims as the counterpart of the absence of any effective Christian attempt to show the falsity of Marxism.

The third odd characteristic of the rapprochement is the absence of any sociological self-consciousness among those taking part. It is after all striking that when Christians did at last in an organized way decide to take Marxism seriously the Marxism to which they addressed themselves was the Marxism of the Communist Parties. For of course the Marxism of the Communist Parties has far less to commend it intellectually than the uncorrupted Marxist-Leninism of the Trotskyist movement or the Marxism of independent politically committed scholars. Neither Mandel nor Lichtheim provides the text which the Christians take to be important. It is easy to see why. The interest of the Christians is not – as we have already noted – in the possible truth of Marxist theory or in separating the truth from the falsity; it is in Marxism-as-the-official-theory-of-the-Communist-Parties. So too the Marxists are interested in theology-as-the-belief-of-the-churches. The participants at the conferences may be intellectuals; but most of them are essentially intellectual organization men, in the sense that they represent the interests of party or church. Hence the lack of any sociological content in the discussions is even more interesting. For the relationships that hold between beliefs on the one hand and forms of organization and of social order on the other go completely unnoticed in these discussions. This aversion from noticing the social role of beliefs must surely itself have a social role.

One final preliminary: conversations between Christians and Communists have been held before and most notably in Germany in the twenties, when 'religious socialism' and the thinking of Bloch and Tillich provided a focus, in England in the thirties, and in France in the late forties. All these encounters had, even within the context of the felt need for political agreement which was urgent in the English and French sample, a polemical character that has now disappeared. Compare *Slant* with *Esprit* (the difference in quality is important too); or compare *Christianity and the Social Revolution*,[5] which appeared in 1935, with the *Marxism To-Day* symposium. To make these comparisons is to bring out the oddity of the present-day discussions even more sharply.

II

Beliefs are not only held by individuals; they can be institutionalized and established as the beliefs of a particular organization or social order. By this I mean more than that a group of individuals holding the same beliefs may band together. I mean rather that a set of interrelated roles may jointly presuppose the truth of a particular belief. All roles do indeed presuppose some beliefs, if only because to specify a role is to specify a set of prescribed or permitted actions which must or may be performed by anyone who is to be recognized as playing that particular role; and every action is expressive of certain beliefs and presupposes others. So if I spray my roses with insecticide or assassinate an archduke my action presupposes a whole web of historical or political beliefs. So too the role of a police officer or of a school teacher will presuppose certain beliefs, both because the actions characteristic of a police officer or a school teacher must do so and because the specification of these actions *as a role* will presuppose further beliefs. An organized set of roles obviously has a certain stability. At the same time it is true that social pressures, unconnected with the beliefs expressed in or presupposed by a given set of roles, may be exerted upon the roles to modify or transform them. When the beliefs are not embodied in the roles, but also held by the individuals whose roles they are, what happens to the beliefs of the individuals? Does the modification of the role lead him to modify or to abandon his beliefs? Or can the new inconsistency between the beliefs embodied in the new role and the beliefs still held by the individual be tolerated under certain conditions?

Consider now a second group of problems. If I as an individual, hold a set of beliefs which are embodied in the role that I play, and these beliefs turn out to be false, what will the consequences for my role-playing be? To suggest the type of answer that would have to be given to this large question, I must first consider the ways in which I can respond as an individual to the discovery that some fact or set of facts is inconsistent with a belief which I have hitherto held, and I can classify these modes of response as either rational or irrational. The rational response to the discovery of facts inconsistent with my belief will be either to abandon or to modify the belief in question, recognizing in each case that I am doing what I am doing. The irrational response to such a discovery will be to attempt to ignore or to disguise the situation, either by acknowledging the newly discovered fact, but covertly transforming the belief so that it is no longer inconsistent with it, while at the same time not acknowledging that the new belief is other than identical with the old, or by refusing to acknowledge the newly discovered fact, maintaining my original belief but deceiving myself and possibly others as to the character of the newly discovered fact. When we have classified these different modes of response, we are in a position to ask about the causes and consequences of some particular individual or group adopting one of them rather than any of the others in the face of confrontation of a particular set of beliefs with a particular set of facts inconsistent with those beliefs.

If we do this we shall want to relate what we say to the problems outlined earlier about role-playing and beliefs. For to ask about the causes and consequences of individuals adopting one mode of response rather than another to the falsification of belief situation will involve asking both about the extent to which the social pressures which modify and transform role-playing produce or favour one mode of response to the falsification situation rather than another, and also about the extent to which a particular mode of response to the falsification situation may engender or favour modifications or transformations in the roles of the agents in question. A good deal of empirical work by sociologists and anthropologists has thrown light on the various forms which the toleration of inconsistency may take and the social structures which are related to these forms; but we possess only one important empirical study which engages with these issues directly, the work by Leon Festinger and his colleagues reported in *When Prophecy Fails*.[6] Festinger studied the reactions of a small religious sect to the falsification of predictions embodied in a millenarian prophecy. His work suggests that it might indeed be profitable to pursue the explanation of features of belief and organization of groups whose beliefs possess or have possessed predictive elements by examining the modes of response to the falsification situation and also the ways in which pressures on the role structure of such groups may engender changes in their beliefs. I now want to suggest that the former type of enquiry may illuminate the Communist attitude and the latter the Christian attitude to the Christian-Communist rapprochement.

III

Begin with the Communists. Although Marx did not date his predictions of the socialist revolution, he clearly expected it within decades. Even well into the twentieth century Franz Mehring could hold that Marx and Engels had been correct in their predictions, but had merely underestimated the time which it would take to realize them. But now consider the situation of Communists in the advanced countries of the West after 1945 (and we ought to note that it is in those countries that Communists have primarily felt the need to engage in dialogues with the churches). They are not like Festinger's sectarians faced with the falsification of a prediction concerning a single, datable event; it has rather been a matter of a long, gradual process in which beliefs could be adjusted to social reality. What type of change is involved?

The perspective of classical Marxism was one in which the actions of the Communist militant were essentially means to the end of revolution. The criteria of right action is precisely whether an action will or will not bring closer a revolutionary situation. An action is judged entirely by its consequences. But the facts of modern industrial society seem to delay the prospect of socialist revolution indefinitely. Thus the problem becomes: what happens to patterns of action of a means-end kind when the belief which embodies and warrants the prediction that the use of these particular means will in fact bring about this particular end is confronted with facts which postpone indefinitely the time when the looked-for end will be realized? The answer seems to be that although the beliefs may still be expressed in forms which apparently preserve the means-ends content of the belief, the actions warranted by and expressive of the belief, will have to be actions performed either for their own sake or for some more immediate end or for the sake of their symbolic significance. The effect of this will be that the formerly held beliefs with their genuine predictive content will come to have a quite different impact. Just this seems to have happened with Communism in non-Communist advanced industrial societies (and in Czechoslovakia, where the effect of Communism has been to produce a somewhat less advanced industrial society than formerly existed).

The actions of Communists are in the first instance forced by social reality into patterns which do not distinguish them from those of many non-Communists. Consider in particular the actions of Communist militants in the Trade Union movement, especially in France and Italy. Ever since the defeat of the PCF's attempt to mobilize the CGT for political action against NATO in the early fifties, the Communist militant has only been able to hold his position of leadership by struggling for the immediate and attainable ends of reformism, wage increases and improvements in working conditions. But in so doing how does he differentiate himself from the non-Communist trade unionist? What significance can his Communist beliefs have for him?

The answer is that they add a cosmic dimension to his immediate activities, but they no longer do so by connecting those activities in a causally effective way to a future revolution. They do so instead by connecting the activities of the trade unionist to other activities which express his immediate moral concern about racism or other urgent threats to human equality. The result is that reformism in the industrial sphere is linked to moralistic idealism in the sphere of human relations. Thus the moralism of contemporary Communism is to be explained as being part of its mode of response to Marxist predictions. Confronted by facts inconsistent with these predictions Communists have resorted to the irrational strategy of transforming the sense of their beliefs so that the beliefs become only very weakly predictive, and yet insisting on the identity of those beliefs with the strongly predictive beliefs which they formerly held.

It is worth noting that it is the same social facts which produce two rather different consequences which in turn unite to produce a new social effect. The role of Trade Union official or shop steward and the role of Communist militant, when these are united in a single individual, will have very different modes of coexistence, depending upon the context in which the individual is operating. In the context of an industrial society in which real wages are growing slowly, but in which inflation is a constant threat, the focus of working-class attention will be on wage demands. The Communist militant's role as a revolutionary tribune of the working-class will be embodied in far less of his activity than is his role as a trade union negotiator. It is not that the latter role will erode or replace the former; it is rather that the former role will become fictional, a matter of dramatic gesture and expressive activity rather than of means-ends activity. Fictional roles are as real as non-fictional, and as liable to have effects in the real social world. But the effects they have are the effects produced by acting a part and these are the effects which depend upon the ability of others to act out counterpart roles and so to take over and respond to gestures. Moreover when we call a role fictional we imply – what is not, or ought not to be, implied when we talk of normal role-playing, in spite of all that Goffmann and Sartre have written – that the agent stands to his role, much as an actor stands to his part; that is to say, we can sharply distinguish the motives and intentions of the individual from the motives and intentions which are embodied in the role.

The social facts which produce this type of transformation of role are the same facts which invalidate the predictive element in classical Marxist belief. The Communist mode of response to this falsification situation, so I have already suggested, is one which coheres well with the transformed role-playing of the Communist militant. He continues to produce an expressive moralism in place of an activist commitment to change intended to be at once immediate and revolutionary. This expressive moralism is Utopian, in Engels' sense of that word. For what Engels meant by 'Utopian socialism' was a socialism that provided no account of the cause and effect relationships which must be relied on in bringing about socialism. Utopianism was always envisaged by Marx and Engels as a religious survival; here no Marxist at least ought to be surprised that a consequence of the transformation of Communists into Utopians is an increased ability and increased desire to communicate with those whose world-view is Christian.

This analysis of course raises more questions than it answers. But it does perhaps suggest some of the questions that need to be answered about the interactions and relationship between changes in roles and role-playing and changes in schemes of belief. Some of the same questions recur in an interesting way if we consider the problem of explaining the Christian participation in the rapprochement.

IV

Christianity had to face the falsification of key predictions in the first century of its existence. The earliest Church believed that the Second Coming of the Lord was sufficiently near at hand to affect immediate planning and calculation. The only immediate and practical way of life was an 'interim ethic', a set of rules for a relatively short period of waiting. When the fulfilment of this prediction was indefinitely delayed, what were the consequences? The Church was forced to confront the fact that Christians had to go on living indefinitely in this world; their religious identity, the role they played as members of the Church, had to coexist with earthly roles. The institutionalization of Christianity had to provide for this co-existence and we find this reflected in a number of different social devices and of corresponding doctrines. The problem is that the eschatological standards of the gospel ethic involve an abandonment of worldly prudence ('Take no thought for the morrow'), the renunciation of power and of economic activity ('Sell all that you have, and give to the poor'); whereas life in the world involves prudence, power and economic activity. One characteristic device for handling this situation is the mediaeval doctrine of the double standard: the monastic abide by the gospel ethic in its immediate form, while the laity only abide by it in attenuated and symbolic form.

The adoption of such devices is and must be characteristic of all those established religions which have institutionalized the prayer, 'Lord, make me fit to enter the Kingdom of Heaven, but not yet'. What happens when a 'church' breeds a 'sect' is that these devices break down, it may be because rapid economic and social change disrupt the socialization process through which people learn to inhabit their religious and earthly roles simultaneously. The sectarian demands that the other-worldly ethics be realized here and now, sometimes restoring as its counterpart and justification the lost predictive element. So the millenarians of the sixteenth and seventeenth centuries. But of course the transition from a stable established complex of church relationships in which the this-worldly order and the other-worldly order coexist to the sectarian process of transforming the this-worldly order into the image of the other-worldly order, because *now* is the time when the prophecies are to be realized, need not be total. The Church has sometimes been able to accommodate movement in sectarian directions, provided it does not go too far. So it was with some mediaeval prophetic movements.

What causes such movement is the need to find more substance in prophetic language than a merely symbolic interpretation (where what is symbolized is not of this world) will provide. Thus if Christians *qua* Christians wish to identify themselves as political agents in the contemporary world they will have to find political structures to which they can point as at least partial realization of the kingdom of God. If this point is to throw light on the attitudes of Christians in the Christian-Communist conversations, then two questions will need answering. The first is why those Christians who do feel such a need feel it now. The hypothesis which I wish to offer as an answer to this question concerns the changes in the role structure of the Christian churches in advanced industrial society in recent decades. The earlier secularization of such societies left for the most part a middle-class laity confronting a clergy whose training, whose career-structure and whose recruitment presupposed an authoritarian and paternalist relationship to their congregations. This relationship was sustained by the status enjoyed by the clergy even among those outside the churches. The erosion of this status has been accompanied by changes in theology and in the theological training of the clergy which mean that the failure of the external world to provide expectations which will sustain their role is matched by the increase of self-questioning required of them. This change in the degree to which the role of the clergy is well-defined has not only as cause, but also as consequence the inability of the laity to play the same parts as before. In particular the increase in the numbers of laity who have higher education and who belong to the first generation to have higher education, even when it is a small numerical factor in the life of the church, produces an important change in the standards which both laity and clergy must use to justify their positions. These standards are provided by the secular world.

The Christians are thus driven simultaneously in two directions. The disengagement from previous role-structures throws them back on the theological specifications of the Christian life in the New Testament relatively unmediated by secondary specifications in terms of contemporary social organization. At the same time the need to find immediate relevance in the formulas of the New Testament results in a need to find earthly exemplifications of the theological *dramatis personae*. This need is met by for example Father Herbert McCabe's identification of the Vietnamese and Cuban revolutions with foreshadowings of the resurrection of the dead.[7] This restores part of the predictive content of the New Testament eschatology; events falling under a certain type of description will, so it is predicted, recur in history. But the description is sufficiently unspecific and sufficiently open-textured for it to be difficult to falsify such predictions. The outcome is a highly qualified millenarianism, the effect of which is to give a cosmic dimension to Christian moral commitment. The abstract benevolence of so much nineteenth-century Christianity is replaced by a more historicist form of moralizing, just as the historicism of nineteenth-century Marxism has been diluted by the new moralism of the Communists.

The second question that would have to be asked and answered is: 'Why it is Communism rather than any other secular movement which provides the earthly exemplification for the theological claims?' Part of the answer may already have been indicated; part, as with all the other questions I have raised, is a matter for further enquiry.

v

Finally I would like, while stressing the tentative nature of my assertions, to suggest that the argument of this paper is important in two directions. I hope that it is clear that in studying the encounter of Christianity and Communism we may throw a sociological light on the development of both, which might not be available to us if we studied them in isolation. It is only where belief-systems encounter other belief-systems that certain facets of their true nature are revealed. Furthermore it is in understanding the relationships between changes in role-playing and role-structure on the one hand and reactions to situations that pose problems for belief that we shall find material for important generalizations. The variety of ways in which the scientist whose hypothesis is put to the test and falsified may respond to this situation have been delineated by philosophers of science. But there are analogues for ordinary non-scientific agents, and the causes and consequences of adopting one mode of response rather than another deserve study by sociologists.

It is impossible for reasons suggested in the second section of the paper to undertake such an enquiry without utilizing criteria of rationality and irrationality to characterize the behaviour of agents. The sociologist therefore cannot enter this field without making judgements about the behaviour of Christians and Communists which appraise that behaviour as well as describe it. It is in this sense that the sociology of beliefs is not, and cannot be, a neutral discipline.

NOTES

1. Versions of this paper have been read to the Dining Group on the Sociology of Religion, Trinity Hall, Cambridge, and to the Research Seminar of the Department of Sociology, University of Essex. I would like to express my gratitude to members of these for a variety of penetrating criticisms.

2. R. Garaudy, *De l'Anathème au Dialogue*, Paris: Plon, 1965.

3. *Dialogue of Christianity and Marxism*, edited by James Klugmann, London: Lawrence and Wishart, 1968.

4. Terry Eagleton, 'Why we are still in the church', *Slant* 14, April-May 1967, p. 28.

5. *Christianity and the Social Revolution*, edited by John Lewis, London: Gollancz, 1935.

6. Leon Festinger and others, *When Prophecy Fails*, Minneapolis: University of Minnesota Press, 1956 (New York: Harper Torchbooks, 1964).

7. Herbert McCabe, *Law, Love and Language*, London: Sheed and Ward, 1968, p. 134.